SHE CAME TO SLAY

ALSO BY ERICA ARMSTRONG DUNBAR

. . . .

Never Caught: The Washingtons' Relentless Pursuit of Their Runaway Slave, Ona Judge

A Fragile Freedom: African American Women and Emancipation in the Antebellum City

When I found I had crossed that line, I looked at my hands to see if I was the same person. There was such a glory over everything; the sun came like gold through trees, and over the fields, and I felt like I was in Heaven.

Slavery is the next thing to hell.

I said to the Lord, I'm going to hold steady on to you, and I know you will see me through.

I was the conductor of the Underground Railroad for eight years, and I can say what most conductors can't say—I never ran my train off the track and I never lost a passenger.

I have heard their groans and sighs, and seen their tears, and I would give every drop of blood in my veins to free them.

I grew up like a neglected weed, ignorant of liberty, having no experience of it. Then I was not happy or contented.

I had crossed the line. I was free; but there was no one to welcome me to the land of freedom. I was a stranger in a strange land, and my home after all was down in the old cabin because my father, my mother, my brothers, sisters, and friends were there. But I was free, and they should be free.

I freed a thousand slaves I could have freed a thousand more if only they knew they were slaves.

SHE CAME TO SLAY

THE LIFE AND TIMES OF HARRIET TUBMAN

God's time is always near. He set the North Star in the heavens; He gave me the strength in my limbs; He meant I should be free.

There are two things I've got a right to, and these are, Death or Liberty—one or the other I mean to have. No one will take me back alive; I shall fight for my liberty, and when the time has come for me to go, the Lord will let them kill me.

ERICA ARMSTRONG DUNBAR

37INK

SIMON & SCHUSTER

New York London Toronto Sydney New Delhi

37 INK
SIMON &
SCHUSTER

Simon & Schuster, Inc.
1230 Avenue of the Americas
New York, NY 10020

First 37 INK/Simon & Schuster hardcover edition November 2019

37 INK/ SIMON & SCHUSTER and colophon are trademarks of Simon & Schuster, Inc.

For information about special discounts for bulk purchases, please contact Simon & Schuster Special Sales at 1-866-506-1949 or business@simonandschuster.com.

The Simon & Schuster Speakers Bureau can bring authors to your live event. For more information or to book an event, contact the Simon & Schuster Speakers Bureau at 1-866-248-3049 or visit our website at www.simonspeakers.com.

Interior design by Jason Snyder
Illustrations by Monica Ahanonu

Manufactured in the United States of America

10 9 8 7 6 5 4 3 2 1

Library of Congress Cataloging-in-Publication Data has been applied for.

ISBN 978-1-9821-3959-9
ISBN 978-1-9821-3966-7 (ebook)

To my father,
Jacob R. Armstrong

CONTENTS

AUTHOR'S NOTE

For Harriet Tubman, one of the remnants of slavery was a recurring headache. Her injury from the blunt-force trauma of a two-pound weight that collided with her skull never went away, and as she got older, the headaches became unbearable. According to her biographers and Harriet herself, she agreed to have brain surgery at Massachusetts General Hospital. In an unbelievable request, Harriet, in her seventies, refused any kind of anesthetic. Like the Civil War soldiers whose hands she had held as they lay injured, she simply asked to bite down on a bullet. As the surgeon sawed upon her skull, Harriet "lay motionless as a log, mumbling prayers through teeth clenched on the bullet."

Looking through the lens of today's medical knowledge, we know that's virtually impossible. *Why the embellishment?* I wondered after I had researched the facts of her life—facts I have conveyed in the pages that follow. Even without this last flourish, she is still one of the bravest, most fearless, committed, and extraordinary Americans of any century. She repeatedly put her life and liberty at risk to rescue others, she worked to advance the rights of women, and she, at the height of her fame and notoriety, risked it all one last time to become a spy for the Union Army. In that capacity, she walked right into enemy territory rather than away from it, because rescuing one or even seventy slaves was like removing a grain of sand from the shore, one at a time. Harriet joined with the Union Army because she understood that only a war could sweep away the entire beach.

So, again, I had to ask myself, why embellish an already extraordinary and singular life? I could only think that Harriet advanced the myth because she worried in her old age (in which she was already struggling physically and financially) that she'd be forgotten. And while that didn't come to pass—there are schools named in her honor, a twenty-dollar bill featuring her likeness slated for eventual production, and dozens of memorials to her—it is true that we have perhaps reduced her. She's remembered, as she should be, as a heroic conductor on the Underground Railroad, but her achievements in women's suffrage and in the Civil War are rarely remarked upon. That she was an entrepreneur, a nurse, a baker, fundraiser, philanthropist, wife, and mother as well is rarely advanced. Here then, presented in a way that I hope is accessible, informative, contemporary, and full of black girl magic, is the multidimensional story of Harriet Tubman Davis, a true boss lady, a superhero, and a warrior.

Erica Armstrong Dunbar

INTRODUCTION

She couldn't remember how many times she had risked her own life to save others. To date, every fugitive she agreed to help escape she had conducted to safety. Her record was sterling. Much was required for the journey—fearlessness, first and foremost. You had to learn to disregard the night creatures, endure the mosquitoes and humidity, and move forward even when a hound's violent bark pierced the night. Driving snow and pounding rain could not intimidate, neither could bruised and bloody feet, nor pitch-black forests. Her resolve and strength were tested each time she traveled back to Maryland on a rescue mission, but she believed in herself and in her God.

It wasn't just Harriet who would need grit. Her fugitive followers would need it too. We can only imagine the orientation Harriet gave the runaways. How she prepared them for what to expect. Her methods had to have been effective, because on her previous trips nothing had gone wrong. But this time, one runaway lost his nerve.

A group of fugitives followed Harriet into the cold swamps of Maryland's Eastern Shore, where they hid during the daylight hours. At night they traveled north, all the while trying to ignore their empty stomachs and deteriorating faith. The journey had taken its toll on the group, but one man in particular was broken by the terror and fatigue. He announced that he would return to the farm and take his chances on the punishment he would likely face. He refused to listen to the other fugitives in his party who begged him to continue on with them. The frigid nights, the wet clothes, the fear, and the thirst wore the man down. He refused to move another step, provoking a standoff between himself and the group's leader. Harriet could not let one man endanger the lives of the entire group. He was the weak link in the chain of coconspirators who now knew the route that Harriet used to rescue her fugitives. She was certain that severe punishment could easily pry this information from his lips. Harriet said, *"if he was weak enough to give out, he'd be weak enough to betray us all, and all who had helped us; and do you think I'd let so many die just for one coward man?"*

She had to protect herself and the others, so she did what needed to be done. Harriet approached the man, aimed a revolver at his head, and told him that he had a decision to make. He could keep moving or he could die. Harriet would kill this man before letting him jeopardize her operation. Not only did she have the well-being of the other fugitives on her mind, but she also thought about the other family members she had yet to rescue. If she had to, she would kill him and bury his body in the woods.

The terrified fugitive knew that Harriet meant what she said. Her eyes warned him not to test her. He made the wise decision to continue on with the other fugitives and to follow his conductor, as others had before him and as others would do after.

Portrait of Harriet Tubman,
Auburn, New York, circa 1868.

PART I
MINTY'S STORY

THE ALPHA JOURNEY

Lying in the belly of the wooden vessel, trying to remember when she had last seen her family, she tried to make sense of the nightmare of her life. It was as if she had stumbled into another world.

Her eyes never adjusted to the complete darkness in the hold of the ship. The smell of stale urine, feces, and rancid vomit swallowed up the breathable air, leaving her nauseated and short of breath. She grew sick; dysentery and smallpox were in the air and claimed the lives of the men and women all around her. Their dead or dying bodies were dragged to the top deck and callously thrown overboard. Their limbs and torsos would serve as shark bait. Though she managed to escape death, she grew weaker.

Rations were limited so she ate stingy portions of the food often stocked for the enslaved: peas, yams, corn, and rice. Meat and fish were in short supply and only eaten by the white men who spoke and moved with rage. Modesty was struck by her own transformation. Her legs in particular were weak, so weak she wondered if they'd even be able to carry her weight or if they would snap and break like dry timber the moment she tried to walk with purpose. If there was one silver lining to her dramatic weight loss, it was that it placed less strain on her aching knees and feet when she was forced to exercise on the top deck. The less jumping and dancing on demand she had to do the better.

It was useless to try and count how much time had passed so she waited—waited for death or deliverance, not knowing if they were one and the same. When the ship finally dropped anchor, she disembarked from her voyage looking like a different person. Her thin and sickly skeletal frame was scarred in more ways than one.

Her eyes met with a foreign land, filled with strange sights and unfamiliar faces. The pale-faced men who had tortured her and her shipmates—those who survived and those who jumped overboard, a not so insignificant act of rebellion—spoke a language that was rough to her ears. She would have to learn this new tongue, and she would need to learn it quickly. Having arrived in the colony of Maryland like hundreds of thousands of other men, women, and children, she was sold to fuel the engine of American slavery. Her enslaver was a man named Atthow Pattison, and once he concluded the purchase, he took her to his farm. He would name her Modesty.

Maybe it was in the blink of God's eye, maybe it took her a lifetime, but eventually she came to understand that she would never again see her homeland or loved ones. She didn't succumb to whatever grief that knowledge produced. Modesty would do what millions of other enslaved Africans fought to do: she survived.

Her strength and will were inheritable traits passed down to her descendants who not only survived but also managed to free themselves from slavery's vice grip. Modesty would not live long enough to witness her granddaughter, Araminta Ross, grow tired of slavery's cruelty. She would never know that little "Minty" would become an American gladiator who fought and slayed the lion known as slavery. Modesty would not live to see her granddaughter change her name and become the "Moses" of her people. She would never know that the name Harriet Tubman would bring hope and strength to the enslaved and raging fury to their enslavers.

This African woman planted a seed of resilience in her progeny that would blossom even in her absence.

• • •

By the time Modesty landed in Maryland, African slavery was well established along the jagged coastline of the colony. Although we don't know the exact year she landed in America, it was most likely sometime during the last few decades of the eighteenth century. Modesty left neither a written record of her life nor did she leave behind an interview. All that existed about her experiences in Africa were passed down through the oral tradition, a form of storytelling mastered by people of African descent. Like the other eighteen thousand Africans shipped to Maryland in the eighteenth century, Modesty probably made a direct voyage from Africa on a British-owned ship.

The majority of Africans who were sold into slavery in the Upper Chesapeake were men, women, and children who hailed from West Africa. Many were kidnapped from towns and villages in present-day Sierra Leone, Liberia, and Ghana. Like Modesty, the enslaved were given new English names. Yet to subvert that erasure, many held on to their customs and traditions by naming their children after the African family members they would never see again.

FIRST GENERATION AMERICAN

Modesty's owner was a member of an established family from the Eastern Shore of Maryland. Atthow Pattison, a farmer who could trace his roots back to some of the earliest settlers in Dorchester County, Maryland, had served in the Revolutionary War, accumulated significant tracts of land, owned seven slaves, and protected his

265-acre farm that sat on the east side of the Little Blackwater River. Modesty lived with the Pattison family, and sometime between 1785 and 1790, she gave birth to a daughter named Harriet Green, affectionately known as "Rit" by her family and "Rittia" by the Pattisons.

We don't know who fathered Modesty's child. Folklore and unsubstantiated accounts state that Rit's father was a white man, but of course, there's no documentation to prove this claim. It is very possible that Modesty was sexually assaulted, perhaps by her owner. As is the case any time there are iniquities in power dynamics within a culture primed to look the other way, rape was an integral part of American slavery, allowing enslavers the ability to impregnate their human property and pad their financial coffers. Whether Rit was the product of rape or of a consensual relationship, we'll never know. Nor will we know Modesty's feelings toward her daughter. She may have worshipped her as her one true thing in the world, or she may have raged against her and everything she embodied, particularly if she was the product of a violation. Or she may have felt a bit of both. But for Pattison, there was less ambiguity. Enslaved babies were as good as gold.

Like millions of others, Modesty disappeared from the record books, leaving her daughter, Rit, and granddaughter, Araminta, to mark her existence.

LIES BUT NOT MISDEMEANORS

There were only a handful of life events that could alter the shape and stability of a family in the eighteenth century. Birth. Marriage. Death. The latter almost always brought deep grief and turmoil. In addition to fear and a sense of vulnerability that accompanied the loss of a young husband or father, family members were often faced with financial questions. Was their financial future at risk or secure? Would they inherit debt or property? And if the latter, what kind of property? Acres of land, livestock, ceramic earthenware, used feather beds? On the Eastern Shore of Maryland, it could be all of the above, as well as human beings. When Atthow Pattison died in 1797, he had every intention of passing on one of his servants, Rit. But there was a catch.

> *"I give and bequeath to my granddaughter Mary Pattison, one Negro girl named Rittia and her increase until she and they arrive to forty-five as would any of her issue born while she was a slave."*

Pattison's will promised something to Rit that her mother Modesty likely dreamed about every day of her life—freedom, even if only eventual. Pattison's actions were not unusual, as slave owners sometimes used their wills to emancipate the dutiful, a kind of incentive: work hard, cause no trouble, and maybe, just maybe, you'll be rewarded. Inevitably, this would have caused Rit unlimited joy, but Rit never learned the truth. Rit's new owner, Mary Pattison, had no intention of ever losing her human property. After inheriting Rit in 1797, she married Joseph Brodess, a farmer with his own land just outside of Bucktown in Dorchester, Maryland, on March 19, 1800. Four male slaves lived at the Brodess farm and Rit toiled alongside them, never knowing that she and any children she might have in the future, had the *legal right* to exit slavery's unrelenting clutch. The Brodess family simply ignored the wishes of the Pattison family patriarch and did what they wanted with their new human property. In their minds, Rit would serve them for the rest of her natural life.

HARRIET'S

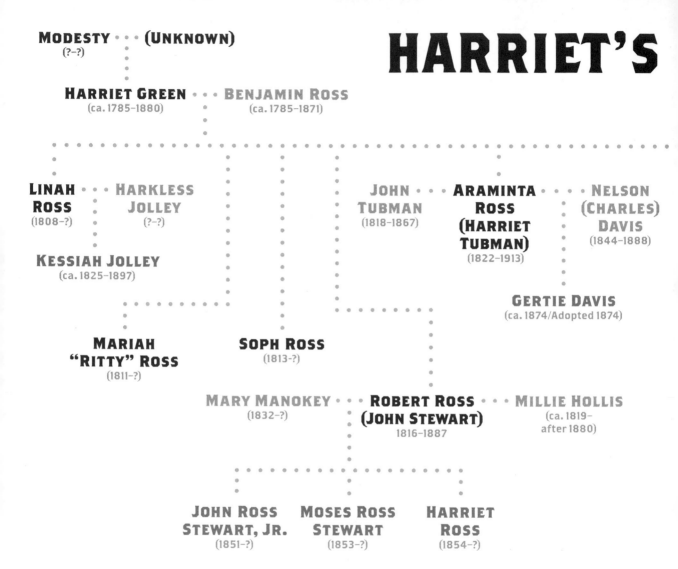

MODESTY · · · **(UNKNOWN)**
(?–?)

HARRIET GREEN · · · **BENJAMIN ROSS**
(ca. 1785–1880)   (ca. 1785–1871)

LINAH · · · **HARKLESS**
ROSS   **JOLLEY**
(1808–?)   (?–?)

JOHN · · · **ARAMINTA** · · · **NELSON**
TUBMAN   **ROSS**   **(CHARLES)**
(1818–1867)   **(HARRIET**   **DAVIS**
                TUBMAN)   (1844–1888)
                (1822–1913)

KESSIAH JOLLEY
(ca. 1825–1897)

GERTIE DAVIS
(ca. 1874/Adopted 1874)

MARIAH   **SOPH ROSS**
"RITTY" ROSS   (1813–?)
(1811–?)

MARY MANOKEY · · · **ROBERT ROSS** · · · **MILLIE HOLLIS**
(1832–?)   **(JOHN STEWART)**   (ca. 1819–
                        1816–1887   after 1880)

JOHN ROSS   **MOSES ROSS**   **HARRIET**
STEWART, JR.   **STEWART**   **ROSS**
(1851–?)   (1853–?)   (1854–?)

Based on the research found in Kate Clifford Larson's *Bound for the Promised Land*

FAM

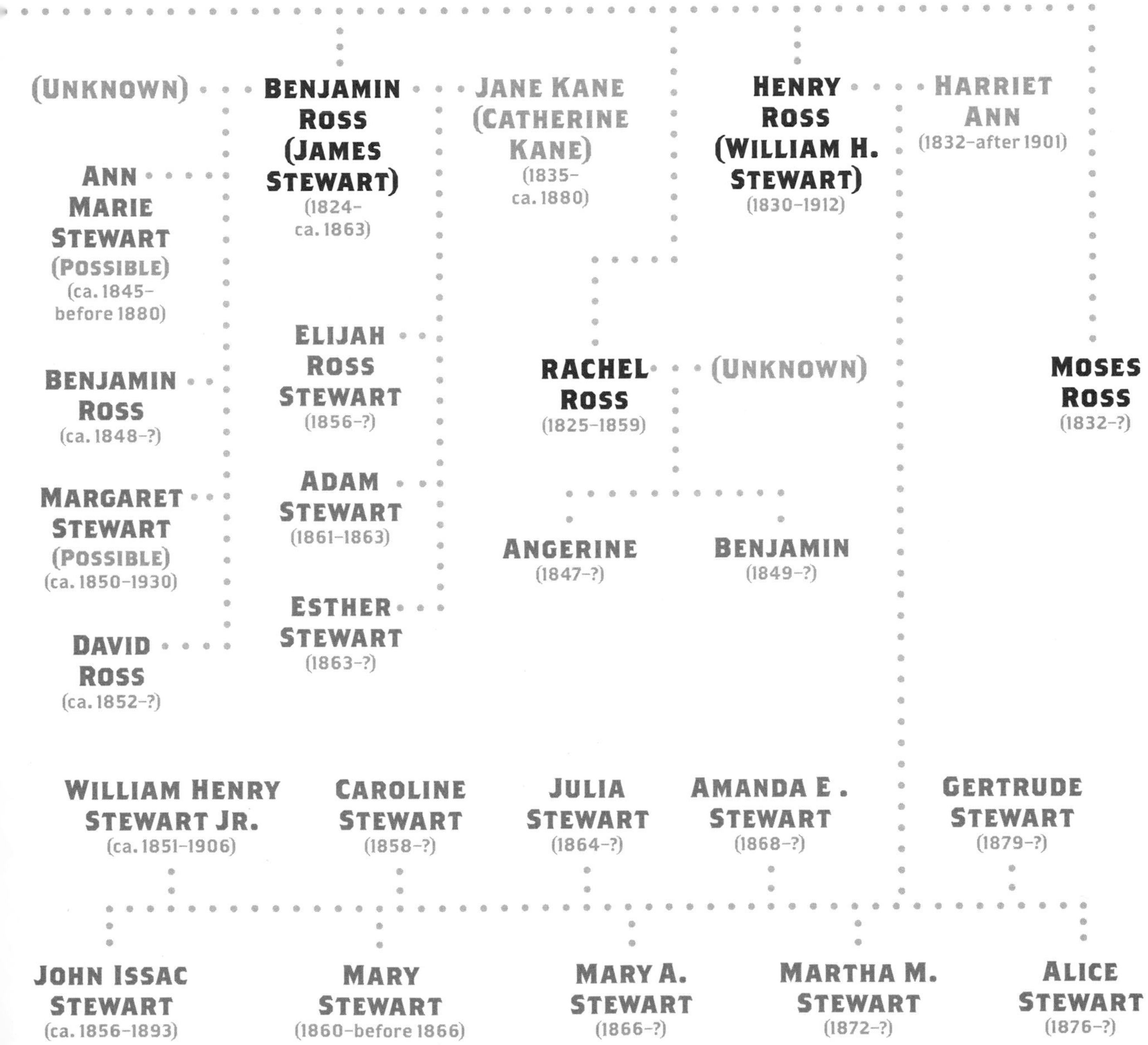

(UNKNOWN)

BENJAMIN ROSS (JAMES STEWART)
(1824– ca. 1863)

JANE KANE (CATHERINE KANE)
(1835– ca. 1880)

HENRY ROSS (WILLIAM H. STEWART)
(1830–1912)

HARRIET ANN
(1832–after 1901)

ANN MARIE STEWART (POSSIBLE)
(ca. 1845– before 1880)

BENJAMIN ROSS
(ca. 1848–?)

ELIJAH ROSS STEWART
(1856–?)

RACHEL ROSS
(1825–1859)

(UNKNOWN)

MOSES ROSS
(1832–?)

MARGARET STEWART (POSSIBLE)
(ca. 1850–1930)

ADAM STEWART
(1861–1863)

ANGERINE
(1847–?)

BENJAMIN
(1849–?)

DAVID ROSS
(ca. 1852–?)

ESTHER STEWART
(1863–?)

WILLIAM HENRY STEWART JR.
(ca. 1851–1906)

CAROLINE STEWART
(1858–?)

JULIA STEWART
(1864–?)

AMANDA E. STEWART
(1868–?)

GERTRUDE STEWART
(1879–?)

JOHN ISSAC STEWART
(ca. 1856–1893)

MARY STEWART
(1860–before 1866)

MARY A. STEWART
(1866–?)

MARTHA M. STEWART
(1872–?)

ALICE STEWART
(1876–?)

DEAR MAMA

By the time Rit was prepubescent, a young girl of ten or twelve, she was considered old enough to complete the tasks we think of, with our contemporary perspective, as more appropriate for grown women. She would've been responsible for the domestic work of the home—cooking and cleaning, tasks that in the eighteenth century required strength and stamina. Every day, Rit rose early to prepare the day's meals. Baking bread and plucking chickens began early in the morning. Washing laundry was often a two-day process that began by soaking the dirtiest of clothing in soapy water or lye. Up to two hundred pounds of firewood was needed in order to heat the water used for cleaning. Rit would've collected water from a well, or a pump if lucky, but most likely, she found her way to a nearby stream and made multiple trips to and from the farm with heavy buckets of water. After scrubbing, wringing, and hanging clothes to dry, Rit would prepare the clothing and table linens for ironing, trying not to burn herself on the flatiron heated by the hearth's fire.

In June of 1801, Mary Brodess gave birth to a son, which only added to Rit's responsibilities as she now also had to tend to the new baby. Young Edward Brodess's arrival was joyful and welcome, but that joy was cut short as some time after Edward's first birthday, his father, Joseph Brodess, died, leaving Mary a widow with a young child.

The responsibilities of motherhood and managing a farm were far too daunting for the new mother. More, she was worried about financial ruin. She needed to remarry and remarry quickly. Mary got the job done. Within a year's time, she wed the widower Anthony Thompson. He would bring his three young sons and nine slaves to the union. For the third time in six years, Rit found herself with a new male owner. As every woman in her same predicament would have had to do quickly, she would learn Thompson's ways, figure out his likes and dislikes and his predilections, and pray that he and his male children would keep their hands to themselves.

• • •

Mary Brodess Thompson's bad luck and despair became Rit's good fortune. Death had ended her owners' marriage, but it led Rit to meet the man who became the love of her life. Ben Ross, one of the nine slaves owned by Anthony Thompson, came to live with this new blended family and he made the acquaintance of a teenaged Rit. We know almost nothing about their first encounter, or how Ben and Rit's love for one another developed. This might have been the very first time that life circumstances smiled upon Rit, reminding her that although trapped in the web of human bondage, she too could carve out a bit of happiness. Rit and Ben chose each other. They would find a way to live, love, and raise a family together, even when the circumstances were challenging. Theirs would be a union that lasted for many decades.

WE ARE FAMILY

Like Rit, Ben Ross was enslaved, but he was a valued timber inspector whose skills were sorely needed on Anthony Thompson's extensive property. Like many other farmers on the Eastern Shore of Maryland, Thompson struggled to stay afloat. Those who worked the land became less interested in planting labor-intensive and soil-depleting tobacco and turned their attention, instead, to harvesting corn and grains. Thompson followed suit and also invested heavily in timber production, an investment that relied upon Ross's skills. When the price for timber and grains bottomed out during the early years of the nineteenth century, however, Thompson was nearly swallowed alive by mounting debt. In 1817, he became one of the many men who faced prison because of his inability to make good on his financial promises. Eventually, Thompson climbed out of his financial black hole, in no small part due to his standing in the community, his race, and his gender.

Nevertheless, this kind of financial instability would have frightened Rit and Ben Ross for they knew that should misfortune strike again, Thompson was not above selling his slaves to make good on a debt. Even more troubling was the death of Mary Pattison Brodess Thompson. Sometime before 1810, the woman who inherited Rit from her father died with her secret intact, never telling Rit that she and any children she gave birth to were to be freed at age forty-five.

Anthony Thompson managed his deceased wife's estate on behalf of her son Edward Brodess, who was set to receive his inheritance when he turned twenty-one years old. Ritt and Ben Ross spent the next decade tending to their children: Linah, who was born about 1808, Mariah Ritty (1811), Soph (1813), and Robert (1816). Some six years later, on March 15, 1822, a midwife was called to Rit's bedside. This midwife would help with the birth of the Rosses' fifth child, and while there is no definitive record of her birth, it is likely that the midwife helped guide Araminta, known as "Minty," into the world. Minty became the newest member of the Ross family. Naturally, they had no idea that this girl child would become one of the most famous figures of the nineteenth century. Born with three strikes against her—Minty was black, enslaved, and a girl—one day, her people would call her Moses.

• • •

Each year that the Brodesses' heir inched closer to his twenty-first birthday, the Ross couple braced themselves for what could become of their family. For many years the Rosses did what few enslaved families were able to do; they stayed together. Like others in their situation, Rit and Ben Ross watched as their children were hired out to neighboring farms to help subsidize the farms and estates upon which they lived. For cash-strapped farmers, this additional revenue stream could keep them solvent. Living apart from one's children exacted a toll, but the Rosses at least knew that their offspring would eventually return. In a world where children were regularly sold away from their parents, Rit and Ben Ross could tolerate their children's situation, that they were enslaved labor-for-hire. It was far better than the alternative.

Meanwhile, the Ross family continued to grow with Ben Jr., arriving sometime in 1823 or 1824. Sister Rachel arrived sometime around 1825, Henry was born in 1829 or 1830, and Moses arrived sometime around 1832, making Rit and Ben Sr. the parents of nine children. Time and again, this family showed their commitment to each other.

Just as the Ross family grew, so too did Edward Brodess's family. By 1824, he married and moved to Bucktown, nearly ten miles away from his stepfather's plantation. He set out to become a farmer in his own right and took his property, including Rit and her children, with him. Ben Ross belonged to Thompson, however, and would have to stay behind in Peter's Neck. When given permission, Ben Ross would have to travel the ten miles by foot or wagon in order to visit with his family. Regrettably, the Ross family fell victim to family separation, a common and merciless attachment of the institution of slavery. But the most devastating blow to the Ross family would land in 1825 with the sale of their second daughter, Mariah Ritty, to a Mississippi slave trader. Only sixteen years old when she was sold, Mariah never saw her parents again. Like tens of thousands of enslaved people in the Upper Chesapeake, Mariah Ritty would most likely end up on a cotton farm in Alabama or Mississippi, hopeful that her teenage memory would retain the names and faces of all she left behind. Minty was a toddler when her big sister was sold and taken away, and while she may not have remembered her face, she would later recall and share the stories of her grieving parents. The grief she witnessed them expressing at losing their daughter would be a motivating and animating emotion for the rest of her life.

CARETAKER

The loss of Mariah Ritty highlighted only one aspect of the difficult emotional work involved in raising enslaved children. Also difficult was the act of watching your babies grow up before their time. Rit was called away from her children for long hours, forced to serve her owner from the early morning hours until late in the evening. With her attention and energy directed elsewhere, she had to rely on her children to raise one another. In her absence, Minty, who was but a small child herself, was placed in charge of the babies in the family. She later recalled:

> When I was four or five years old, my mother cooked up to the big house and left me to take care of the baby an my little brother. I use to be in a hurry for her to go, so's I could play the baby was a pig in a bag, and hold him up by the bottom of his dress. I had a nice frolic with that baby, swinging him all around his feet in the dress and his little head and arms touching the floor, because I was too small to hold him higher.

As a five-year-old, she would work to keep her younger siblings out of harm's way, making certain that they ate, slept, and played under her watchful eye. A child tasked with raising babies, Minty may have been overwhelmed at times. But the responsibilities also prepared her for her future role as rescuer-in-chief of members of her family.

• • •

When Minty and her family moved with Edward Brodess to Bucktown, they discovered that the new farm was relatively small. With few livestock and not enough work to keep all of the enslaved busy, Brodess did what many slave-holding small farmers did: he rented out his slaves. Minty was one of the first to go, as it wasn't financially prudent to keep her on his own farm, so he hired her out to a nearby farmer. She was no longer baby Minty, she was now a slave who would be forced to learn new skills—in this case weaving and serving a family that would make demands on her twenty-four hours a day.

FLESH FOR RENT

Although she was not the first of her parents' children to be hired out, Araminta's departure reminded them of what little control they, or any enslaved parents, had over the lives of their children. Her father, Ben Ross, was ten miles away on the plantation he was bound to, and was already at a disadvantage when it came to protecting his family. Rit didn't have much sway either. It can be imagined that all she could do was gather herself, dispense words of wisdom and encouragement to her young daughter, and advise her on everything from how to carry herself to how to stay out of the way, complete her duties, and avoid the whip. These hushed words would've fallen upon immature ears. Araminta was not yet six.

Hired out to James Cook and his wife, Araminta arrived at the farm, nervous and somewhat disoriented. Later in her life Araminta described the scene,

When we got there, they was at table eating supper. I never eat in the house where white people was and I was ashamed to stand up and eat before them.

• • •

She soon learned the breadth of her new responsibilities: muskrat trapping, house-keeping, and weaving—so different from Brodess's farm. Her new world, one that was startling and odd, was terrifying for a young child. She came to understand the new habits of her temporary owners, but she never grew accustomed to the work that was expected of her. Araminta had to grow up quickly; her childhood was over.

Many farmers on the Eastern Shore of Maryland saw muskrat trapping as a way to not only provide food for their families but also as a means to supplement their income by selling the pelts. Muskrats burrowed into the banks of streams and rivers and built nests to protect themselves and their young from cold weather and predators. James Cook set muskrat traps along his marshy property line and required Araminta to check the traps and collect the dead rodents. This task would be difficult for a child with small hands and underdeveloped strength, and it was made all the more miserable because the water along the Eastern Shore of Maryland remained cold for a good part of the year.

During her time with the Cooks, Araminta developed a cough and runny nose. If her employers hoped it was a common cold, they were quickly disabused of this notion. Soon, flat red spots appeared on her face and hairline, moving down her neck, back, and across the lower part of her body. Then, the high fever struck, leaving her weakened body racked by chills and aches. Although she had come down with the measles, her owner didn't see this as a reason to excuse her from work. Measles or not, she was still expected to wade through frigid waters to check on the muskrat traps, to complete her work as if she were healthy. Araminta's condition grew so debilitating, she was eventually unable to complete her assigned tasks. James Cook likely complained to Edward Brodess, fussing that his hired slave could not perform

Young Minty

her duties. He may have even threatened Brodess with the charge of breach of contract. Araminta was finally sent back to the Brodess farm where her mother cared for her daughter—trying desperately to nurse her sick child back to health while still tending to her own assigned tasks. Araminta did finally grow strong enough to return to the Cook farm, but she wouldn't stay there for very long. Over a number of years, Brodess hired Araminta out to multiple people. She would go from farm to farm, never knowing what kind of abuse or danger she might encounter.

Back on Brodess's farm, Araminta had helped to care for her siblings, but she did not know how to take care of a nineteenth-century home. There were skills required to be successful with this work, skills that Araminta had not yet learned. And when she arrived at a new home to which she had been leased—Miss Susan's—she proved just how inept she was with domestic work. For example, Araminta didn't know to open the windows before she began her dusting and sweeping. Although she worked diligently, the dust Araminta worked so hard to remove simply resettled throughout the house. Her mistakes infuriated Miss Susan, who in turn punished Araminta for such infractions. She removed the whip from her mantel and beat Araminta on her head, face, and neck. When she wasn't cleaning the house, she was forced to take care of Miss Susan's baby. Araminta was still so small that she would have to sit on the floor when holding the baby. Although she was a child, Miss Susan turned over most of the child-rearing responsibilities to her. *"An that baby was always in my lap except when it was asleep, or its mother was feedin it,"* Araminta later recalled.

She was forced to work nearly twenty-four hours a day. At night, she was required to tend to the baby, to rock its cradle and prevent it from crying out and disturbing its mother. By day, an exhausted Araminta spent her waking hours cleaning the house and caring for the baby. Not unexpectedly, she often drifted off to sleep in the middle of the night, a rest that only lasted until Miss Susan, who slept with a lash underneath her pillow, would wake her with the sting of her weapon, splaying open the flesh on Araminta's neck and head.

Eventually, the sleep deprivation and the beatings proved too much to bear. Araminta decided to run away, and hid in a neighboring farm's pigpen. Runaways would often take to the woods and abandoned farms to experience momentary peace from an angry owner's abuse. Araminta preferred to sleep with pigs than in the house with Miss Susan, and she lived among the livestock for five days, battling with a large sow for scraps of food. Starvation and thirst were often responsible for the eventual return of fugitives. Araminta was no exception in this regard.

I was so starved I knowed I'd got to go back to my Missus, I hadn't got no where else to go, but I know'd what was coming.

Just as she predicted, Araminta was beaten upon her return, but her experience in hiding marked an important moment in her young life. Even as a child, Araminta's natural response to the brutality of slavery was to run. She knew the consequences would be painful, but she was willing to face them head-on.

• • •

Having struggled with trapping first and now domestic work, Araminta returned to the Cooks and this time, she tried her hand at weaving. The incredibly difficult work of weaving required patience and excellent fine motor skills, as weavers handled large looms with pedals, battens, and reed combs. It was complicated work, and the Cooks expected Araminta to make everything from clothing to rugs on their large loom. Perhaps she was simply too small to work the handloom, or maybe she had trouble learning how to pass the shuttle back and forth between the yarn threads. Whatever the reason, Araminta never learned to weave. Domesticity wasn't for her.

The Cooks were through with her. Once again, they sent her back to Brodess who, still in need of the extra income, hired her out to another temporary owner, a person Araminta would only refer to as the worst man in the neighborhood. It was the fall season and this time she was assigned to agricultural work, specifically to harvest flax in the fields. Many farmers on the Eastern Shore of Maryland planted flax, a crop that could be transformed into linen once it reached the textile mills of New England. Flax could also be used to make grain bags, wagon covers, and sails for ships, but harvesting flax was no easy venture. Planted in the spring, the crop was typically prepared for harvest in the late summer or fall when the woody-stalked plant reached three feet in height. Araminta would pull the stalks from the earth, bundle them, and prepare them for drying. The seed removal was a difficult task often given to male slaves. The flax was dragged through a hetchel, a cluster of long spikes that were nailed through a wooden board. After the seeds were collected, the stalks were moistened and allowed to rot so that the breaking process could commence. Araminta would swing a heavy board to break the husks of the flax in order to expose the fibers that were eventually spun into thread.

This work was tough, and the conditions were harsh and unrelenting. But despite the minimal rations, temperatures that reached well above one hundred degrees in the height of summer, and disease-carrying mosquitoes, there was one development that would prove beneficial in later years. Araminta's body transformed into a sinewy machine of muscle and strength. Breaking flax and hoisting heavy sacks onto wagons reshaped Araminta's adolescent body such that it could eventually compete with even some of the enslaved men on the farm. It was hard work—back-breaking work, but Araminta preferred toiling in the humid and hot sun of summer fields over her previous work in the house. To toil within a household was to always be on duty, never free from reprisals. Life under the constant and watchful eye of a foul-tempered owner meant never-ending misery. The fields and the woods, alternatively, offered protection from constant monitoring, if nothing else. The outdoors, which she grew to love, became her sanctuary.

HEAD TRAUMA

On occasion, Araminta was relieved from the responsibilities of the field in order to complete chores or small tasks. Sometime between 1834 and 1836, Araminta and an enslaved cook from the same farm were sent on an errand for what was supposed to be a quick, uneventful trip to the store to pick up a few items needed for the house. But when Araminta crossed paths with a young man from a nearby farm, her life was profoundly changed.

An overseer was in hot pursuit of the man who had the audacity to abandon his post, as if he were free. And his pursuer had every intention of whipping him. Tension was palpable within the walls of the store. The overseer ordered Araminta to help tie down the enslaved man, but she refused, allowing the slave the opportunity to slip out of the store. In a fury, the overseer picked up a two-pound weight off the counter and hurled it in the direction of the runaway. Araminta's head received the full force of the iron weight instead. The impact broke her skull, as she later recalled.

It cut a piece of that shawl clean off and drove it into my head. They carried me to the house all bleeding and fainting. I had no bed, no place to lie down on at all, and they lay me on the seat of a loom, and I stayed there all that day and the next.

Just like the time she contracted measles and was forced, nonetheless, to continue working, Araminta returned to her toil in the fields without ever being treated for the life-threatening injury, even as she bled from the festering wound and grew weaker by the day. *I went to work again and there I worked with the blood and sweat rolling down my face till I couldn't see.*

• • •

Eventually, Araminta was returned to the Brodess farm, not for rest and recuperation, but so that her owner could attempt to sell her to the highest bidder. Of course, no one wanted to buy a slave that appeared to be on death's door. Not only was she weakened, she was plagued by headaches and sleeping spells, which would suddenly subdue her and which she could not control. She remained in her sickbed for months, adjusting to the unpredictability of her new symptoms. Araminta would fall into a deep sleep in the middle of a thought or a conversation, a sleep from which she could not be roused. Though in the 1830s there was no fancy term to describe Araminta's condition; her grave head injury likely induced a form of epilepsy that was accompanied by seizures. Even without a formal diagnosis, her friends knew that when her head dropped and she lost consciousness, all was not lost. Eventually, she would awaken.

This permanent side effect from her head injury was disabling for sure, but there was an upside: it was accompanied by a religious awakening.

INNERVISIONS

Her recovery from a fractured skull appeared to be a miracle. The physical transformation was accompanied by a metaphysical one as well. Perhaps her near-death experience pushed her into the arms of Christianity, or maybe the constant violence and trauma of slavery made Araminta depend upon the hope and optimism that was tied to faith. Now a devout Christian, she believed that her sleeping spells served as a portal to her almighty.

Araminta would wake from her spells with memories of visions and images that predicted the future. These dreams would serve as signposts, directing Araminta's actions, literally, for the rest of her life. These directives became critical when she began her work on the Underground Railroad. Her dreams would tell her which roads to follow in the dark hours of the night and alert her to people and places to avoid. Araminta's informed intuition could help her stay two steps ahead of an owner or slave-catcher that meant to do her harm, and her visions helped her better protect her family and loved ones.

Her visions were hers alone, but her body was still controlled by her owner, who hired her out to a man named John Stewart. Now a teenager, she was sent back to work in the fields. She later described the backbreaking work she was assigned as, *"The rudest of labors,—[I] drove oxen, carted, and plowed and did all the work of a man."*

• • •

As her health improved, however, Araminta took pride in her physical strength, which once again grew to be quite robust. She began work on the timber gang, chopping wood and hauling heavy loads to nearby wagons, all to the delight of her white owners. Araminta gained a reputation for her reliable work in the fields and the woods, and while the work was grueling, it kept her close to nature, that sanctuary of refuge and comfort. Another added benefit was that Araminta's new work assignment brought her in closer proximity to her father. During her five-to-six-year stay at John Stewart's farm, Ben Ross continued laboring as a timber inspector. His owner had promised to set him free at the age of forty-five and miraculously, this promise was kept. Ben Ross became a free man in 1841.

It's natural to assume that Ben Ross's emancipation gave him reason to celebrate, but what did it mean to live as a free person surrounded by slavery? Yes, he was free, but his wife and children were not. Every time he watched Araminta drive the oxen and split wood, he remembered that her labor was not her own, and there was little he could do to protect his daughter from exploitation. While his freedom offered advantages, it would never give him the same privileges of white men. Paradoxically, Ben Ross's free status highlighted his powerlessness. His freedom was a reminder of his family's enslavement.

THE ULTIMATE LOSS

Around the same time that Ben Ross was emancipated, the Ross family would once again fall victim to the ultimate viciousness of slavery. With agony and despair, Rit and Ben Ross watched as two of their daughters, Linah and Soph, were sold out of state. Struggling farmers would erase debt or simply turn a profit by selling young enslaved men and women farther south, where a market hungry for enslaved bodies devoured human property. Cotton plantations were spreading like wildfire across the South and west of the Mississippi. Linah and Soph were most likely doomed to a life of gang labor—growing and picking cotton morning, noon, and night. Sold for four hundred dollars, Linah was led away in handcuffs and placed in jail until her sale was complete. Her two children, Kessiah and Harriet, were left motherless. When her irons were removed, she cried out, "Oh my children! My poor children!" Soph, her sister, may have been sold with her child, but the records are not clear. Linah and Soph, like their mother and siblings, were supposed to be set free by the age of forty-five, but Brodess, like his mother before him, paid no attention to his grandfather's will. He illegally sold the two women, leaving a devastated family to pick up their shattered hearts and figure out how to live with the deepest of emotional scars. With the profit, Brodess purchased additional land.

Though she never saw them again, Araminta wouldn't forget the sisters who were stolen and then lost to the slave trade. This kind of trauma affected enslaved people in different ways, making some turn to religion, while others became emotionally vacant, with a sworn aversion to emotional ties. For others like Araminta, it made the desire to marry and build a family ever more important. Like Mariah, the first sister to be sold, Linah and Soph would never be replaced, but Minty attempted to construct a family of her own and would pray that they would be spared the same fate as her sisters.

SAY HER NAME

At some moment during the early 1840s, Araminta met John Tubman, a free man of mixed race who lived near her father in Peter's Neck, Maryland. Very little is known about Tubman, except that he lived among the growing number of free blacks—between 30–40 percent of the black population in Dorchester County. Their union was a reflection of her quiet charisma and her ability to draw people to her, for it was dangerous and disadvantageous on Tubman's part to marry a woman in bondage. Although their union would never be legally recognized, enslavement was inherited through the status of its women, so any children John Tubman fathered with Araminta would follow in their mother's footsteps. By uniting with Araminta, Tubman's future children would be the property of the Brodess family and vulnerable to cruelty and sale. When the couple married in 1844, Tubman's love for her trumped his concern about his future children.

After the marriage, Araminta adopted her mother's first name (Rit was short for Harriet), took her husband's last name, and began calling herself Harriet Tubman.

LOVE AND MARRIAGE

Their honeymoon was short-lived, as the tension in their marriage began relatively early. For one, John Tubman never took Harriet or her visions very seriously. After a disturbing sleeping spell, Harriet would share her concerns with the people closest to her. Sometimes her premonitions made her fear for the safety of herself and her family, but John Tubman often poked fun at what his wife called her visions, suggesting instead that she was foolish and even mentally challenged. He may have also resented how his wife made and spent her money. Over time, Brodess stopped trying to find farmers willing to rent his enslaved woman and instead, he struck a deal with Harriet. She paid Brodess an annual fee (fifty to sixty dollars) that allowed her to select her own work assignments. This arrangement not only allowed Harriet some control over her life, but it also meant that she would not always live on the same farm as her husband. The separation may have engendered an unbridgeable divide. On the other hand, it allowed her to make additional money, funds that could be saved and used however she chose. She might have contemplated purchasing her own freedom someday. Instead, Harriet did what few enslaved people had done before: she took her extra money and hired a lawyer to fight for her right to be free.

• • •

Harriet must have had a suspicion about her mother's status—suspicions fueled either by oral history, whispers about Rit and her children's promised freedom, or even a vision that came to her during one of her sleeping spells. Whatever the inspiration, Harriet saved enough money to pay an attorney to scour the available legal documents concerning her ownership. What the lawyer uncovered was devastating. Harriet learned that freedom had been kept from her mother for more than a decade and that her sisters had been sold off illegally. Finally, she understood that she too was promised emancipation upon her forty-fifth birthday, none of which mattered. The Brodess family did not adhere to the law, and there was nothing that an enslaved man or woman could do to contest their actions. The law would rarely entertain, let alone acknowledge, the complaints of human chattel. Harriet had paid good money for the truth and now that she knew about the decades-old lie, there was no way to reverse the years of lost labor, and more devastating, the sale of her three sisters. Her resentment was hard to swallow.

That Harriet and John Tubman never had children together would likely have also contributed to their problems. Perhaps her years of illness and abuse affected her fertility, or maybe she made a purposeful decision not to have children while still enslaved. After all, Harriet knew that if Brodess would not acknowledge her or her mother's promised freedom, he would never acknowledge that of her children. Many enslaved women used herbs and roots to prompt miscarriages or prevent themselves from ever becoming pregnant. On the mornings she woke from a shared bed, Harriet could have brewed herself a cup of cotton root tea to ensure that the love she shared with her husband would not bear fruit. Their relationship surely suffered for multiple reasons, the specificity of which are lost to time. But the odds, given all the aforementioned reasons, were against them.

Approximately four years into their troubled marriage, in the winter of 1848–49, Harriet fell ill, rendering her unable to work with any regularity. Of course, Harriet cherished the independence work afforded her, as well as the money, but she had a more dire concern. Brodess was in serious financial trouble. He was looking to sell a few slaves and Harriet knew that because of her illness, she was at the top of his list. Harriet prayed for him. She never believed Brodess to be a true Christian, but she hoped that if Brodess accepted God into his heart, he would repent for his sins and perhaps become a better man, maybe even see the inhumanity in selling her. With God in his heart, maybe he would even consider honoring the will that would free her family.

During her prayer vigil, however, rumors reached her that with his financial problems growing more imminent, he planned to quickly sell Harriet and some of her brothers to the lower South, a landscape painted black and white with the expansion of black slavery and cotton blossoms. She altered the tenor and directives of her prayers. *"I changed my prayer, and I said, 'Lord, if you ain't never going to change that man's heart, kill him, Lord, and take him out of the way, so he won't do no more mischief.'"*

THE AUCTION BLOCK

On March 7, 1849, Edward Brodess, only forty-seven years old, died. Harriet's immediate reaction to the news was pure joy. Her prayers had been answered—another reminder that God heard her cries and protected her from evil. But her joy quickly evaporated. Brodess's death only exacerbated the family's financial problems. The newly widowed Eliza Brodess had to raise money to pay off her late husband's debts and she would have to do it quickly. Selling off a few of her slaves would alleviate the financial strain and bring her account books in order. Harriet recalled, *"Next thing I heard old master was dead, and he died just as he lived. Oh, then, it appeared like I'd give all the world full of gold, if I had it to bring that poor soul back. But I couldn't pray for him no longer."*

Harriet and her family waited and worried. They went about their normal tasks, but their minds always returned to their vulnerability. Who would be sold and where would they go? The questions were soon answered when Harriet's niece, her namesake, and her two-year-old daughter Mary Jane were sold to a local merchant for three hundred and seventy-five dollars.

Harriet understood that the sale of slaves would continue until the widow Brodess was debt free with enough funds to support her family. The moment of reckoning had come, and Harriet knew that she, still recovering from her illness, was more than vulnerable, more than likely to be the next person to climb upon the auction block. She refused to let this happen.

By twenty-seven years old, Harriet had lived a difficult life. The viciousness of slavery had tested her in ways that were almost unimaginable. Her childhood had been stolen when she was made to care for her younger siblings while her mother worked. She was abused, beaten, disabled, and forced to do the most difficult farm labor possible. Her family had been torn apart when Mariah Ritty, Linah, and Soph had been sold. And Harriet knew that the Brodess family would never make good on the will of the elder Atthow Pattison. The memories of empty muskrat traps, back-breaking housekeeping, and flax harvesting fanned a seething anger. Her rightful emancipation at age forty-five would never materialize.

THREE HUNDRED DOLLARS REWARD.

RANAWAY from the subscriber on Monday the 17th ult., three negroes, named as follows: HARRY, aged about 19 years, has on one side of his neck a wen, just under the ear, he is of a dark chestnut color, about 5 feet 8 or 9 inches hight; BEN, aged aged about 25 years, is very quick to speak when spoken to, he is of a chestnut color, about six feet high; MINTY, aged about 27 years, is of a chestnut color, fine looking, and about 5 feet high. One hundred dollars reward will be given for each of the above named negroes, if taken out of the State, and $50 each if taken in the State. They must be lodged in Baltimore, Easton or Cambridge Jail, in Maryland.

ELIZA ANN BRODESS,
Near Bucktown, Dorchester county, Md.
Oct. 3d, 1849.

The Delaware Gazette will please copy the above three weeks, and charge this office.

Runaway reward advertisement for Tubman (Minty and her two brothers). Cambridge Democrat newspaper, October 3, 1849.

She would have to wrestle it away from the widow who planned to line her pockets from another slave auction.

On September 17, 1849, Harriet and her two brothers, Ben and Henry, would try to preempt the widow's plans for them. The three siblings took off, and by October, Brodess's widow had placed an advertisement in the newspaper for the threesome, offering a reward of up to one hundred dollars for each of the runaways.

The stress and the fear proved simply too much for Harriet's brothers, and the siblings began to bicker over directions, which was further complicated by their illiteracy. After two weeks in the woods, Ben and Henry began to change their minds, wondering if the fear that prompted them to run away was rational. Ben had left behind his wife and children, a betrayal that may have become too burdensome to carry. Water and food supplies would have been scarce, and long black nights hiding among the trees would bring insect bites and unwelcome encounters with wild, nocturnal animals. The brothers knew that they would be punished if they returned to the Brodess farm, but perhaps they would only be sold to a local farmer, and would still be able to see their families. Among the thickets, the brothers searched for and clung to optimism, that no matter how bad a beating they suffered, it was better than the unknown. Their sister had other plans. She too had left behind a husband, a set of parents, siblings, and all that she ever knew, but there wasn't enough guilt or fear to make her return willingly to her owners. Not anymore. Ultimately, Harriet's brothers disregarded her feelings when they made the decision to return. They were willing to face the consequences of their departure and they would compel their older sister to join them. Ben and Henry dragged their sister back to the farm. This would be the last time that Harriet let a man control her movements.

When she returned, Harriet listened to the hushed words and quiet tones in which her enslaved friends reported that she and her brothers were to be sold immediately.

She had no time to hesitate. *"I had reasoned this out of my mind; there was one of two things I had the right to, liberty or death; if I could not have one, I would have the other."*

Sometime after October 3, 1849, Harriet set out by herself on the path to freedom. Her decision to travel alone allowed her to make her own decisions and to trust her instincts and the God that never betrayed her. Standing only five feet tall, Harriet harnessed the strength that had come from years of chopping wood and driving oxen. She could not read or write, nor did she have a compass to help guide her, but she knew about the North Star, and it would prove to be enough.

SHE'S OUT

The details surrounding Harriet's escape are not well known. Most fugitives kept secret the names of friends and allies who assisted in their escape as the long arm of the law threatened fines and imprisonment to all who helped enslaved runaways. Federal laws forbade the harboring or assisting of any enslaved fugitive and anyone who offered help to Harriet or any other runaway could face dire repercussions. But Harriet had faith and knew that her God would not forsake her. Her first blessing appeared in the form of a woman.

It is possible that the woman—whose name is lost to posterity, if it was ever known to Harriet—was a Quaker. Members of this Christian sect were considered allies to the enslaved, and luckily for Harriet, the Eastern Shore was teeming with them. As pacifists, they opposed war, and a core-defining element of their brand of Christianity affirmed that everyone, enslaved or free, possessed the light of God. For nearly a century, Quakers openly opposed slavery and joined with the earliest antislavery societies along the northeast seaboard.

Harriet confided in her new ally and received valuable information about people she could trust on her long journey north. As a gesture of appreciation and a token of payment, Harriet gave the woman a bed quilt, a memento that held tremendous emotional (and some small monetary) value for the fugitive. It was one of the few ways that a person like Harriet could repay people willing to risk their livelihood on a runaway. Even though Harriet had hired herself out to work and had saved some of the money that her labor generated, it is unlikely that she had a significant amount of cash on hand. The woman took Harriet's quilt as the payment and sign of appreciation that it was and offered her a slip of paper with the names of two people who would help her on the journey to freedom. When the woman's husband returned home he placed Harriet in a wagon and after nightfall, transported her to another safe house that would provide shelter, information, and advice.

This would be her second stop on what had already become known as the Underground Railroad, the loose connection of safe homes, businesses, barns, and structures that could be found throughout the nation and were prevalent throughout Maryland and Delaware. Although there had long been people who decried and condemned the system of slavery and committed themselves to helping runaways, the Underground Railroad became well known in the 1830s, and took its name from the rise of the railroad system that began to lay its metal tracks across the nation. The stations, also known as depots, could be large or small and were run by stationmasters. Those who helped fugitives travel from place to place were often called conductors; other allies donated food and clothing to help fugitives contend with cold Northern winters or to help them blend in with local communities. For runaways like Harriet, shoes and clothing were not to be taken for granted. Many fugitives had never owned a pair of shoes and often arrived at the doors of stationmasters with tattered and ragged clothing, a dead giveaway of fugitive status for relentless slave-catchers and bounty hunters.

SAY HER NAME

Araminta Ross

Minty

Harriet Tubman

Harriet Tubman Davis

Moses

A Black She Moses

General Tubman

Mother Tubman

Harriet was different from most fugitives: she was a woman. The majority of enslaved people who took to the woods, marshes, rivers, and streams were young men who made the agonizing decision to leave behind their loved ones for a chance at freedom. For young women, the realities of enslavement kept them tethered to small farms and large plantations. It was difficult for young fathers to leave their children behind, but like Ben Ross, many did not live with their nuclear families, perhaps making escape just a little less painful. Most young women between the ages of fifteen and thirty-five, on the other hand, were bound to reproduce often, so as to steadily grow the slave labor pool. For most, they'd be physically bound to their children by the need to breastfeed and care for them throughout much of their reproductive years. Enslaved women who lived with their babies and young children also knew that should they run away and leave their children behind, they might be targeted for a vindictive owner's lash. The thought of possible mistreatment of their offspring often kept enslaved mothers from running away. The alternative was to try to escape with a child in tow—an almost impossible feat. Tiny babies cried out from hunger pains and discomfort, alerting slave-catchers to their whereabouts. Small children had a difficult time keeping up with the fast pace of foot travel, slowing down a mother on the road to freedom. There were many reasons that mothers refused to take a chance on escape, but most of them centered on their children.

Harriet did not have to worry about the pain of abandoning babies or attempting to travel with them. Her marriage to John Tubman had not yielded any children, and while it might have been a source of deep pain for the couple, it turned out to be a blessing—one she wouldn't fully realize until she made the decision to escape.

We don't know the exact route that Harriet traveled on her first departure from Maryland. We do know that she found her way through two states and over 120 miles before she reached Pennsylvania: the first Northern state that had turned its back on slavery. Much of her journey would be made at night, following the North Star and the guidance of newly acquainted friends. Each step that Harriet took, each wagon that she hid in, and every barn and structure that offered refuge, presented both hope and fear. Fugitives never knew who was trustworthy, and although Harriet believed that her God would rescue her, the journey was perilous. Traveling north with nothing but a star and bits of guidance from strangers was far more than risky; it was a journey that was almost certain to meet with failure. But like her grandmother Modesty, Harriet beat the odds. The adversity she had confronted for decades prepared her for the most difficult moment of her life. The cruelty and intense labor of slavery strengthened her body and her resolve, allowing her to endure the long and dangerous trip to Philadelphia. Her connection with nature, which she developed while being forced to labor outdoors, also became essential to her success.

We don't know the exact day that she crossed over the Pennsylvania state line in the fall of 1849, but what we do know is that it was a moment of mixed emotion for Harriet. She felt ecstatic, no doubt. But also lonely. Isolated, she confronted the new realities of her arrival in the City of Brotherly Love: *"There was no one to welcome me to the land of freedom. I was a stranger in a strange land; and my home, after all, was down in Maryland; because my father, my mother, my brothers, and sisters, and friends were there. But I was free and they should be free."*

Wondering how to move forward without her family, who were still living in daily jeopardy, she made a decision that may have appeared irrational, but one that set her apart from other fugitives. She wouldn't leave her family and friends in bondage; she would find a way to rescue them. After taking the time needed to gather the strength and resources to willingly walk back into the jaws of slavery, Harriet returned south.

PART II
SHE AIN'T SORRY

The Conductor

THE CONDUCTOR

When Harriet arrived in Philadelphia, it was unlike anything she had ever experienced in her life. Crowded with people and more geographically sprawling than anything she had witnessed in the small county of Dorchester, Philadelphia was a major port city with a large and well-established free black community. Slavery had existed in Pennsylvania but slowly, the state began to wean itself from the human bondage. By 1849, there were no slaves living in Philadelphia (and nearly twenty thousand free blacks). Harriet had lived among free blacks on the Eastern Shore of Maryland, but something was very different about free black life in her new city. While free black men and women were still stationed at the bottom of the economic ladder, there was opportunity. Black entrepreneurship laced the small streets of the city where men and women sold fruits, vegetables, and oysters to anyone who wished to purchase. Mother Bethel African Methodist Episcopal Church stood at Sixth and Lombard Streets, reminding Philadelphians that black people were central to the lifeblood of the city.

While there was a growing black middle class, Harriet knew, nonetheless, that she would be locked out of most employment opportunities. There were no agricultural jobs for her in the city. Moreover, her illiteracy kept her from the higher-paying and respected jobs. Consequently, she found herself trapped in low-paying domestic work, a situation that would never promise stability, let alone wealth. This was the very kind of work from which she had run when loaned out to Miss Susan, the very kind of labor at which she was so inept. But what was a fugitive to do? Harriet had to shake her dislike and adapt to her new environment. She could not be picky. With the city's abundance of cheap Irish and black labor, Harriet was competing for jobs in one of the toughest domestic-service markets in the nation. Her options were limited but she managed, most likely with tips from new acquaintances, to pick up work in private homes and hotels. During the summer months, she traveled to the resort town of Cape May, New Jersey, to make extra money from vacationers. Like other fugitives, she would have asked new friends—free black people—for tips about what meals to prepare for her white employers, and she would have to learn the customs and expectations for service.

Harriet was well aware that slave-catchers were always on the prowl, but she soon learned that the federal government would join in their treachery, making life on the run even more difficult. In 1850, the Fugitive Slave Law passed through Congress granting new enforcement to a law that had existed for more than half a century. The law made it harder for runaways to slip anonymously into Northern states. For people like Harriet, freedom became a virtual impossibility in the United States. Enslavers had the support of the federal government, and with it, they sent their unscrupulous bounty hunters to search through Northern city streets and rural farms to locate and capture their runaways.

Like other fugitives, Harriet began to contemplate a move to Canada, one of the only true safe havens for runaways. But before she could finalize plans to travel north, terrible news found its way to Harriet. She learned from her network of new friends in Philadelphia and others she had met in Baltimore and Delaware that her family members were now in imminent danger.

Given the debt still outstanding on the Brodess ledger, Harriet knew that it was a simple matter of time before the widow would sell one of her family members, and in December of 1850, Harriet learned that her niece Kessiah was slotted for the auction block at the Cambridge courthouse. This wasn't the first time that Kessiah had been scheduled for sale. In the past, Kessiah's free husband, John Bowley, managed to outmaneuver her owner. This time, there was little that he could do. When Harriet learned what was to transpire, she must have immediately thought about her sister Linah—Kessiah's mother—who was sold and then taken down South. Would two generations suffer the same fate?

Now there was a goal that served as a counterweight to that feeling she faced when she made her own escape, the feeling that as welcome and wonderful as freedom was, contentment was still out of reach as long as her family remained in bondage. She was determined—despite the risk attached—to travel to a Southern state where patrollers were newly empowered, ready to pounce upon and return any fugitive who had a handsome bounty attached to their head, to save her niece and her two children from the fate that befell her three older sisters. Harriet mustered up her courage and traveled back to Maryland, this time to Baltimore, to help rescue the doomed woman.

Harriet probably didn't imagine herself as a leader. She was a black woman of small stature—the least respected or protected person in the United States of America. But the moment she began that journey to Baltimore, she began a transformation. No longer was Harriet one of the lucky ones who escaped from bondage; she was now a soldier in the war against slavery. Harriet knew that she could be apprehended and returned to the Brodess farm, but she didn't let fear consume her. She would have taken her cues from the black women in her family—Modesty and Rit—who sacrificed and stood strong in the face of adversity. She would do the same. To survive slavery, one had to think strategically, anticipate their owners' moods and next steps, and develop the physical strength required for field and domestic work. Each time Harriet cleared small trees from the land or hoisted heavy sacks of flax onto wagons, she grew stronger. With each trip to the well, Harriet's muscles developed, allowing her to carry the heavy buckets of water necessary for washing laundry. Ironically, slavery's burdens—all that she suffered while working with different yet demanding families—turned Harriet into a warrior, a warrior who was ready to slay the dragon of human bondage.

• • •

As soon as she arrived in Baltimore, Harriet located her brother-in-law, Tom Tubman, who placed his own life in jeopardy by hiding Harriet and gathering intelligence to plan for Kessiah's escape. He relied upon the networks that supported black fugitives all over the nation, networks that Harriet would rely upon for more than a decade. With Tom Tubman's help, and in conjunction with Kessiah's husband, Harriet devised a risky plan. The details were not written down—this kind of information could land Kessiah's friends and family in jail, or worse—but instead whispered and dedicated to memory by trusted allies.

When the day of the sale arrived, Kessiah and her children, James Alfred and Araminta (Harriet's namesake), stood in front of a crowd of anxious customers. At slave auctions, potential buyers had the right to inspect the bodies of anyone up for auction. Prodding fingers checked mouths looking for decayed teeth and other evidence of illness. Enslaved women were often examined without their clothing, giving male buyers an opportunity to assess and judge their genitalia. The crowd knew that Kessiah was able to do the one thing that all slave owners wanted—she could have children. The evidence of this stood by her side awaiting their fate, praying they would be sold with their mother. Every newborn enslaved baby offered additional wealth to owners and, at only twenty-five years old, Kessiah still had years of childbearing ahead of her.

Once the bidding ended, Kessiah and her children were taken from the steps of the courthouse and put into confinement as the auctioneer went to enjoy a quick meal. When he returned, he realized that something had gone terribly wrong. The human property was gone. John Bowley, Kessiah's free black husband, had secretly placed the winning bid on his family and managed to smuggle his wife and children out of Dorchester County via boat, ferrying them the ninety miles to the bustling seaport of Baltimore. Harriet then rushed her fugitive family into hiding, allowing her niece and her niece's children to collect themselves and prepare for the journey to Philadelphia. It was winter, and Kessiah's six-year-old son and newborn baby would make travel slow going, but Harriet made certain that her family arrived safely in Philadelphia.

With her kinfolk in the North, Harriet was no longer alone. She finally had family members who could share in her joy and help ease the loneliness she felt in the new, still-foreign city. Her successful mission offered Harriet more than companionship; it also gave her confidence. She now knew that her escape was no fluke, that she had the skills to rescue others. Perhaps this was the moment that Harriet understood her calling. She could use her networks and knowledge of the roads and byways between Maryland and Pennsylvania to rescue more family members. Her visions and God's protection could turn what seemed impossible into a reality. It might take many years, but Harriet intended to rescue her entire family.

Within a few short months, Harriet was once again called to assist her family, and sometime during the early months of 1851, she returned to Baltimore for a repeat performance. Through a similar network of allies, Harriet rescued her brother, probably Moses, and two other young men, and as she did with Kessiah, she led them successfully to freedom.

Within eighteen months of her own escape, Harriet had rescued six people from the violence of slavery. Her victories made one thing clear: she was now a tested conductor on the Underground and her reputation as such would begin to grow. Her successes in Baltimore also likely emboldened her to believe that she could rescue people from the Eastern Shore of Maryland. But Harriet was no fool, and she knew that slipping in and out of rural Maryland would prove much more dangerous than her missions to Baltimore. She also knew that the only way to convince and collect her family members, especially her husband, was to go directly to them. It had been nearly two years, but Harriet retraced her steps back to Dorchester County. Her exact routes and modes of transportation were never recorded, but most assume she slipped into the Eastern Shore by boat and by foot. She had her God, her courage, her visions, and the love of her family to guide her back into the belly of the beast called slavery. To see her husband again and to bring him to Philadelphia was worth the risk.

BETRAYAL

It was the fall of 1851, and it may well have taken a week or longer for Harriet to travel back to Maryland. The orange-and-red leaves of the maple trees had already turned brown and fallen, creating a cacophany of sound with each of her steps. The seventy-five-foot-tall white cedar trees that lined the swamps and marshy areas of the Eastern Shore hid Harriet from sight as she made her way toward Dorchester County. Unpredictable impediments like bad weather or reports of lurking slave-catchers would force her to hole up in safe houses or hide in the wilderness until the threats disappeared. The familiar smells of pig

farms and barren cornfields reminded Harriet that she was home.

Dorchester County, Eastern Shore, MD.

She must have looked forward to the reunion with her husband. Though she had left John Tubman behind, and though their marriage had its share of troubles, they were still family. After all, her own parents had modeled familial commitment, and she had never shed her love for or sense of allegiance to him. She imagined that once the two were reunited, they would leave the South and start fresh.

When she arrived in Dorchester County, she immediately went into hiding, but sent word to John Tubman that she had returned for him and that he should prepare to travel north with her. Harriet waited for a response, and when it finally came it was not what she expected to hear. Her husband had moved on with his life and had no interest in seeing Harriet, let alone leaving his home. After Harriet's escape, he no doubt assumed that he would never see his wife again. With neither children nor a wife to answer to, Tubman hit reset on his life and married another woman, a free black woman named Caroline.

When he learned that Harriet had returned for him, he not only refused to even see her, he made certain that Harriet knew about the new love in his life. Any children he had with Caroline would be free-born and he would never have to worry about the sale or escape of his wife or children.

Pained by her husband's response, Harriet felt betrayed, dejected, and defeated. She had risked her life for this man, only to find out that she had been replaced. Gradually, whatever feelings of sadness or hurt she felt were quickly replaced by rage. Eager to confront her husband and his new wife, Harriet was ready to fight.

Later in her life, Harriet reflected back upon this painful moment, admitting that she had every intention of upbraiding the man she now saw as a cheat. She planned to approach the new couple's cabin and "go right in and make all the trouble she could." But a cooler head prevailed. Harriet realized she could not risk her own safety with a physical confrontation that would certainly bring unwanted attention and possibly capture. She was upset but she wasn't stupid. *If he could do without her, she could do without him,* Harriet realized. She let John Tubman go.

EXPATS

Rejection was difficult for Harriet, but her personal turmoil did not alter what she realized was her true calling. Her former husband may not have joined her, but her dangerous trip to the Eastern Shore would not be in vain. Harriet was in a position to help many other people, both family and friends, and she transformed the pain and anger she felt into a motivating force. She took from Dorchester County what was most important to its white farmers—their labor—and shepherded them to freedom.

Harriet left Dorchester County, but returned in a few weeks and gathered a party of eleven enslaved men and women and fled. This trip was different for Harriet and the others, because the final destination was not Philadelphia. The Fugitive Slave Law of 1850 made residency in Northern states a risk not worth taking. Even though she could not read the newspaper, Harriet was familiar with the new enforcement of the law, and refused to rescue a group of eleven fugitives only to lose them to slave-catchers in Northern cities. Philadelphia was no longer far enough north, and the same held true for New York City and Boston. There was, however, one alternative that could offer freedom and stability to those on the run. In her own words, *"I wouldn't trust Uncle Sam with my people no longer, but I brought 'em [clar] off to Canada."*

Slavery's grasp was so powerful that it forced Harriet and those who followed her to leave a country they called their own. While they may not have been designated as citizens of the United States, Harriet and her party of eleven would now be fugitives *and* expats. The details are hazy, but Harriet probably led her party to Philadelphia and then took the train to New York City. From there they would have traveled to Albany or Rochester, New York, one of the last stations on the Underground before crossing into Canada. The size of Harriet's party was quite

"HARRIET'S MOVES"

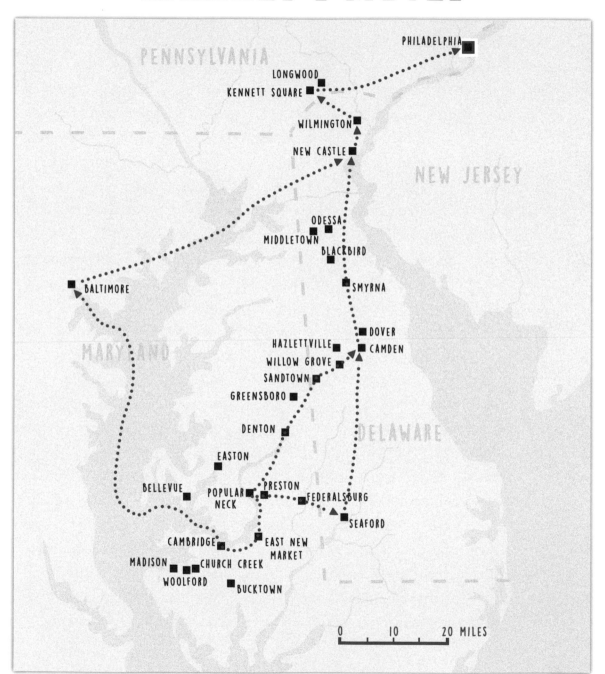

TRAVELING THE UNDERGROUND

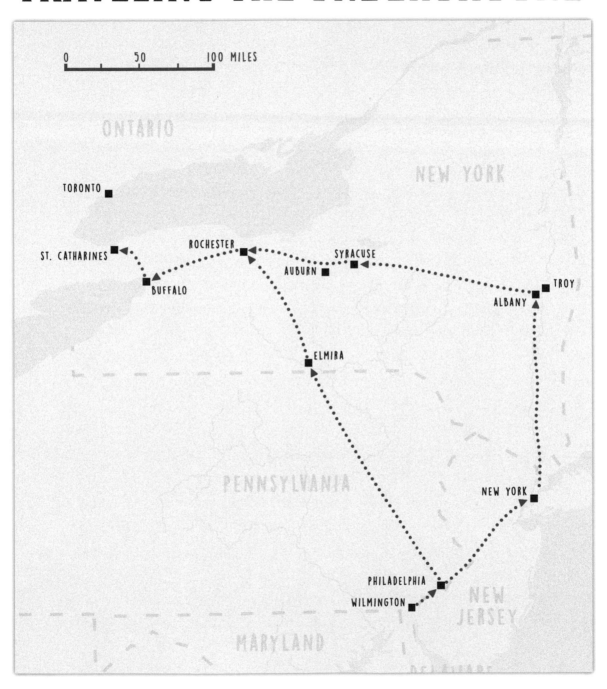

large and unusual, and it would've been difficult to find discreet lodging for so many runaways. It is likely that for this trip Harriet called upon the aid of one of the most well-known antislavery activists of the era for help: Frederick Douglass.

Like Harriet, Douglass was born on the Eastern Shore of Maryland, and he too had been rented out to farmers. One of them, Edward Covey, was notorious for his cruel and inhumane treatment. Douglass moved to Baltimore where he learned to read and write, and similarly to Harriet, he fell in love with a free person. Anna Murray would help Douglass escape, eventually following him north to become his wife. Douglass's powerful story and oratory skills landed him on the antislavery lecture circuit. By 1845, he published his book, *Narrative of the Life of Frederick Douglass, an American Slave*, which quickly became a bestseller in the United States. In his autobiography he wrote, *"On one occasion I had eleven fugitives at the same time under my roof, and it was necessary for them to remain with me until I could collect sufficient money to get them on to Canada."*

Frederick Douglass never mentioned the names of the fugitives who looked to him for assistance, but it is certain that the two most famous runaways from Maryland crossed paths during their fight against slavery.

Harriet's group arrived in Ontario, Canada, during the frigid winter season, and while life would be far from easy, Harriet and the others were finally free. Canada was not without its problems, but it offered more protection from Southern slave-catchers than cities such as Philadelphia or New York. On occasion, bounty hunters would sneak across the border with the goal of retrieving fugitives, but this hazard was far less common than it was in the United States, providing them a measure of safety.

They settled in the city of St. Catharines in Ontario, a community filled with fugitives who, like Harriet, understood that Canada offered opportunities. Fugitives

Harriet Tubman and Frederick Douglass

found their way down unpaved thoroughfares lined with businesses—some owned by people who looked like them. They encountered black tradesmen who had perfected their craft as barbers, dressmakers, blacksmiths, and coopers. And, in the open-air market, black merchants—men and women, young and old—signaled to potential customers, artfully displaying their wares in individual stalls. Among the vendors, black women in wide-brimmed straw hats, some of whom had been fugitives themselves, haggled with patrons over chickens, bacon, butter, and a wide variety of fruits and vegetables. Black soldiers patrolled the Welland Canal while black deck hands unloaded cargo from a steady stream of ships that shuttled between Lake Ontario and Lake Erie. The possibilities for employment and progress must have excited the fugitives. These markers of hope and advancement kept the new arrivals optimistic, even when times grew difficult.

Many runaways eventually found work as laborers and servants for affluent families or as cooks and maids for local hotels. But getting their new lives on track would prove far from easy. When Harriet and her followers arrived at St. Catharines they were without proper food or clothing to get them through the difficult winter. They struggled to find housing and security and were relegated to the same kinds of difficult agricultural and manual labor that they knew all too well, except this time, they had to complete their tasks in blinding snowstorms and frigid temperatures. They tried to ignore the prickling feeling in their fingers and toes as they chopped wood in the icy forests of Ontario, but surviving the cold proved extremely challenging. Their exposed faces left noses and cheeks vulnerable to frostbite as they chopped and collected cords of wood to be sold at market. Frostbitten toes and ears turned white and quickly developed fluid-filled blisters that burned like fire. The fugitives would have learned that in severe cases, frostbite could turn the skin black and deaden the tissue. Toes and fingers would simply fall off, leaving a person disabled for life. These were hard lessons to learn, lessons that might have made the runaways reconsider the journey they'd made from the Eastern Shore.

Homesickness presented these new Canadians with another set of challenges. Memories of parents, children, spouses, and friends who remained in Maryland haunted the men and women who took a chance with Harriet, and they mourned their losses while balancing new survival strategies. They also had to embrace the reality that they were free from slavery but still bound by racism, which caused Harriet and her band of newcomers to tread lightly on their new land. But here's how we know that they wouldn't trade anything for their journey: No matter how homesick, tired, regretful, or hungry they may have been, none of them ever returned to the farms that exploited their bodies as beasts of burden. Harriet stated later in her life: *"I have seen hundreds of escaped slaves, but I never saw one who was willing to go back and be a slave."*

• • •

Harriet remained with her brother in St. Catharines during the winter of 1852, surviving the season with the help of local friends and allies who were committed to helping fugitives. Her niece Kessiah, whom she had rescued, and Kessiah's husband, John Bowley, also left Philadelphia and traveled north to resettle in Canada with their family members. By the spring, Harriet had recovered her energy and was ready to head back to the United States to make some money and plan additional trips back to Maryland. Her network in Philadelphia helped her find work, and she headed back down to the resort town of Cape May, New Jersey, to work as a cook for wealthy white families. Once she had saved enough money and the autumn leaves had started to fall, Harriet planned her next rescue, and returned to the Eastern

Shore of Maryland yet again. We don't know the names of those she helped, but Harriet returned to Canada with nine more fugitives.

This became a pattern for the conductor: she would work during the summers and save as much money as possible, and at some point during the fall she would travel back to Maryland to save another group of runaways. By 1854, Harriet had made at least five trips back to the Eastern Shore and had rescued close to thirty enslaved people. During the winter, the conductor pulled off one of her most daring rescues; she arranged to bring her brothers Henry, Benjamin, and Robert Ross out of slavery and to the safety of Canada.

WHO YOU GONNA CALL?

Her brothers were habitual escapees. It had been five years since Harriet first left Maryland, and during those years all three of her brothers made repeated attempts to escape, none of them successful. Ben and Henry must have regretted their decision to give in to fear back in 1849. If they had followed their sister's lead, if they had traveled with her to Philadelphia, they would have avoided the past five years of enslavement and the beatings that inevitably accompanied every unsuccessful attempt to flee. Over the years, the situation grew more dangerous for Harriet's brothers, and as the winter months of 1854 approached, everything came to a head. The Brodess widow was tired of the Ross brothers and their repeated attempts at escape, so she decided to sell the three siblings during the Christmas holiday. As there was little time to spare, Harriet had a letter sent to Jacob Jackson, a free black man in Dorchester County. In the letter, Harriet embedded hidden messages to her brothers stating that they should be prepared and ready to step aboard when *the good old ship of Zion comes along.* Although the letter was inspected by the postal authorities, it raised no suspicions, and Harriet was able to get news to her brothers that she would soon come to their rescue. She planned their escape carefully, choosing Christmas Day for their departure date. This was the most opportune time for the brothers to escape, as the pace of work over the holiday was often slowed, allowing the enslaved to visit and celebrate the holy holiday with one another. This fleeting Christmas joy was often followed by mass slave sales at the beginning of the year, sales that would eradicate whatever debt the enslavers had accumulated that year. And in this case, the Brodess debts continued to mount.

The siblings were to meet at her parents' cabin and from there, Harriet, her brothers, and a small number of enslaved friends would begin their journey out of slavery. Family history reports that Harriet and her brothers had their father blindfolded and brought to them as they waited in a nearby building. Harriet's father was blindfolded so that if asked whether he had seen his children, he could honestly answer no. Harriet had not laid eyes on her father for five years, and for a few glorious moments she had an opportunity to talk to her daddy. It's easy to imagine that she promised to return for him one day, but in that moment she had to save her brothers from certain and immediate danger. As for her mother, the siblings decided it was best not to involve her, however painful. They took hold of their father's arms and *he accompanied them some miles upon their journey. They then bade him farewell, and left him standing blind-fold in the middle of the road. When he could no longer hear their footsteps, he took off the handkerchief, and turned back.*

● ● ●

Over the next few days, Harriet and her party made their way to Wilmington, Delaware, and connected with Underground stationmaster Thomas Garrett. He provided Harriet and one of her companions with new shoes because they "had worn their shoes off their feet." Once they had eaten and rested, they were sent to a home in Chester County, Pennsylvania, and from there they were shuttled to William Still's office in Philadelphia.

From 1849 to 1860, Harriet continued to risk her life for the sake of her family and loved ones who remained in slavery's grasp. Of the thirteen trips she made back to Maryland, each one was demanding and tested her will and resolve in new ways. Aside from avoiding slave-catchers, Harriet had to boost the confidence and tenacity of fugitives, convincing them to stay the course should their commitment waver. It was difficult to escort a large party of runaways through the swamps and mountains, but that was often how Harriet conducted business. She always led her expeditions at night, using the stars to guide her in the dark woods, trying desperately to avoid the dangers of nighttime travel. Accidentally stepping on a copperhead snake could be deadly, and coyotes and wolves made their presence known as they hunted for prey. Harriet carried a pistol for protection, and she wasn't afraid to use it on a wild animal, a slave-catcher, or a renegade runaway.

SHE CAME TO SLAY

Each and every day there were new challenges to confront. To throw bounty hunters off their tracks, Harriet would often disguise herself as an old woman or dress in men's clothing. More than once, she came face-to-face with previous owners and each time she outmaneuvered them. On one occasion, Harriet found herself sitting near a former owner while riding on a train. If she made any sudden moves or attempted to leave, she would've drawn attention to herself, so she quickly picked up a newspaper and hid behind it, pretending to read while carefully concealing her face.

Always quick and clever, Harriet trusted her own decisions, but when it came to the care of her fugitive followers she had to be creative. As she made her way toward the figurative Canaan, Harriet relied on visions that emerged from her sleeping spells. The sense of danger, of what to avoid, and who and what to trust was presaged by her visions, which she believed unwaveringly. When she awoke from one of her sleeping spells, Harriet often recounted images and visions that would aid her and the other fugitives in their flight. She would sometimes even translate these visions into song, alerting her charges to possible danger by the words and tempo of a selected spiritual. Though they trusted their "Moses," these seizures, nonetheless, could rattle their confidence. For Harriet, however, these sleeping spells were reminders of her faith and trust in God; he would always show Harriet the way, even when she couldn't see it herself.

As difficult as adult fugitives were to lead, small children and babies were even more challenging to rescue. Crying newborns could instantly reveal a party of fugitives, but Harriet couldn't ask fugitive mothers to leave their children behind. She had to figure out how to stop the crying. There was one way, and she often availed herself of the opportunity: drugs. Medicine was still unsophisticated in the 1850s, and many medications possessed trace amounts of opium. Paregoric was a medication used to treat asthma, diarrhea, and coughing fits, and mothers rubbed the gums of teething babies with this powerful tonic. It was Harriet's go-to as well. She administered higher doses to infant fugitives, making them fall into a deep and undisturbed sleep. Once unconscious, Harriet placed the babies in a basket and kept the party moving forward. Another benefit of the medication was that it was an appetite suppressant, which helped small children deal with the meager rations available to fugitives.

The hunger, the frigid temperatures, and the poorly fitting shoes that gave rise to blisters and bloody feet were just a few of the challenges faced by the men and women who escaped bondage. Though Harriet's own threshold for pain was unusually high—a testament to her strength and endurance—she was not impervious to pain and upset. Her body also wore the scars of multiple trips to Maryland: her cuts and bruises served as badges of honor.

FEARLESS

Harriet's strength was inordinate, but on occasion she took ill after difficult travels. On one harrowing trip, she was leading four men out of Maryland, but about thirty miles from Wilmington, Delaware, she became unsettled. Harriet listened to her body and sensed danger before it became catastrophic. Her fluttering heart always notified her when something or someone was a threat; she believed it was a message from God. She abandoned the road and came upon a stream, but without a bridge or a boat, the fugitives would have to cross the water by foot, a terrifying prospect for the men in her party. Harriet entered the frigid water, but the men refused to follow, waiting to see if their leader could make it safely to the opposite bank. Fearlessly, Harriet waded through the shoulder-high water, but she was never submerged. Only when they witnessed her successful crossing did the men agree to follow. They crossed a second stream and finally found their way to the home of a black family that gave them food and shelter while they waited for their wet clothes to dry. Harriet had no money to pay the family, but she couldn't let their kindness go unnoticed. She turned to the woman of the family and offered her undergarments (valued possessions at the time) as a gesture of appreciation. Harriet literally gave the clothes off her back in order to lead the party to freedom.

When she finally arrived in Delaware, Harriet was so ill that she could barely speak. The frigid water and inclement weather had taken its toll on her body. In the past, she'd struggled with upper-respiratory infections, and now a similar ailment returned with a vengeance. Unfortunately, it wasn't the only thing that plagued her. During the journey, Harriet experienced discomfort in her mouth. The debilitating pain grew worse until eventually, it became intolerable. A trip to the dentist was out of the question. Most people in the nineteenth century avoided the dentist altogether as rudimentary techniques and indelicate tools ensured a painful experience that left toothless smiles. Enslaved people and fugitives went through the entirety of their lives without ever having dental care, leaving exposed cavities that led to excruciating nerve pain. Harriet would have tried to soothe her toothache with natural remedies, but the pain persisted and pushed her to make a drastic decision. She couldn't allow the pain to interfere with her rescue mission, so she decided to eradicate the agony the only way she knew how: she needed to remove her own tooth. Reports regarding her tooth extraction vary. Some say she used a rock and others mention the butt of a gun, but one way or another, Harriet used blunt force to knock out her own front teeth. Her missing teeth became legendary, erasing any doubts about Harriet's fearlessness, her strength, and her endurance.

• • •

Fear of both the unknown and the certain weighed heavily on the minds of the men, women, and children who gathered up their courage and made the desperate lurch toward freedom. The unknown took the shape of pitch-dark woodlands, ice-cold caverns, and abandoned barns that served as shelter from icy rain and heavy snow. Fugitives never knew if supposed allies would prove honorable when faced with danger or if they would tremble and cave when confronted by vicious slave-catchers. Not knowing when or how they would eat or drink, or how long it would take to walk hundreds of miles, could paralyze a runaway before they even left their own county.

But the knowable kept tired fugitives on the move. Everyone understood what happened when an attempted escape ended in failure, an outcome that would be brutal and traumatizing. Blood soaked the earth where runaways were whipped within an inch of their lives. Repeat offenders were tied down and prepared for the excruciating pain that came with the amputation of a foot. And for many, the physical punishment was just the beginning of the torture. Slaveholders leery of losing money cashed out on their risky investments. Still bleeding from open stripes across their backs, fugitives were sold farther south to suffer on cotton and rice plantations until the end of their days.

Running away was a harrowing ordeal for anyone to experience once in his or her life, but Harriet elected to make this journey more than a dozen times. She knew the risks involved, but every year she would lead at least one party of runaways out of Dorchester County, Maryland. She had rescued most of her family but not yet her parents. The circumstances now forced her hand.

Ben and Rit Ross must have felt a sense of relief each time one of their children disappeared into the woods with their sister. While they would have worried about their safety, they knew their children were in good hands with the daughter who had successfully rescued one sibling after another. Although her father was a valued timber inspector, the slave owners who lived on nearby farms grew suspicious of his actions. As a free man, some began to think that Ben was integral in the disappearance of the enslaved on the Eastern Shore, especially since a disproportionate number of them were his family members. Accusations of his involvement grew stronger, and word spread that Ben was going to be arrested by local authorities. His freedom and his connection to Harriet were liabilities. Rit was also a free woman, not because the Brodess family adhered to the will that mandated her emancipation at forty-five years of age, but because Ben finally convinced the Brodess widow to sell his wife to him for twenty dollars.

Once Harriet learned of the danger facing her parents, she made an unusual springtime trip back to Maryland in 1857. The threat of her father's imprisonment and recent political events created a new sense of urgency to rescue her parents. Although they were free, Ben and Rit had no rights or protection, a situation that was enforced by the highest court of the land. Around the same time that Harriet was planning to leave for Maryland, the Supreme Court finally weighed in on the most contentious political debate of the century. Chills ran down the spines of fugitives and free blacks upon hearing the words of Chief Supreme Court Justice Taney as he and the majority of the Supreme Court ruled that no person of African descent was entitled to the status of citizen. Without citizenship status, free blacks were pre-empted from legal protection and, worse yet, the court decided that slavery could take root in *any* state in the nation. Confining slavery to the Southern states was deemed unconstitutional, a victory for slaveholders and a nightmare for free blacks and runaways. Harriet knew there was no time to waste; she had to get to her parents.

Ben and Rit were in their seventies—extremely elderly by nineteenth-century standards—and a trip to Philadelphia and then Canada had to be planned differently, because they would not be able to withstand the same level of exhaustion and discomfort as younger runaways. Fragile health was common for elderly ex-slaves, and arthritic knees and low endurance would add days, if not weeks, to the trip north. To compensate, Harriet found an old horse and attached a makeshift rickshaw that would carry her parents when they were unable to walk. But this improvised transportation prohibited Harriet from following the same routes she had used in the past. She could not lead a horse through marshy swampland and jagged terrain at night; she would have to rely on more even ground to secure her horse's footing. This brought Harriet and her parents in closer contact to open roads and with it, the possibility of discovery.

On June 4, 1857, despite the risks, Harriet and her parents arrived at the home of Thomas Garrett in Wilmington, Delaware. From there, they traveled to Philadelphia to meet with William Still, one of Philadelphia's most dedicated stationmasters on the Underground. Although the Rosses were technically free, their arrival in Philadelphia was a marker of success. They traveled farther north to Rochester, New York, where they stayed with one of Frederick Douglass's close associates for a few weeks before finally arriving in St. Catharines, where Ben and Rit Ross were finally reunited with their children, and met new members of the family who were born during the years of separation. Ben and Rit shed their former surname and, like their sons, adopted the last name of Stewart. What appeared unimaginable eight years earlier was now a reality. Their immense elation would only be tempered by the memories of the daughters lost to the cotton plantations of the Deep South and the one who remained in Maryland.

• • •

After her parents arrived in Canada, Harriet made her way back to the Eastern Shore for another unusual rescue. Her sister Rachel and her two children were still enslaved, yet the planning of this escape proved extremely difficult. Rachel did not live on the same farm as her children, making communication almost impossible. Harriet remained in hiding while she tried to devise a plan, but the pieces failed to fall into place. Never content to rest on her laurels, she nonetheless rescued others on that trip; still, her inability to bring Rachel and her children to Canada must have felt like the biggest of failures.

Tubman Conveying Her Parents out of Slavery

ANTISLAVERY AGITATOR

Having rescued most of her family, Harriet decided to travel less frequently. Though she offered advice and aid to dozens of other runaways who used her escape routes and safe houses on their flights from slavery, Harriet needed to tend to other concerns. Her aged parents were safe in Canada, but survival was difficult as cash was in short supply. Shifting her attention from rescuing the enslaved to sustaining her family, Harriet began to focus her energies on raising money and resources.

As an illiterate black woman, Harriet's employment opportunities remained limited, but because of her rising fame among antislavery groups, she learned that she could raise funds by simply telling her story. Throughout 1858 and 1859, Harriet traveled across New England speaking at antislavery events, as had Frederick Douglass, William Wells Brown, and Solomon Northup. Their experience as enslaved people and as fugitives were authentic, giving white Northerners a front row seat to Southern slavery. Audiences were both captivated and mortified by what they heard. For them to hear firsthand accounts of what living as chattel was like made slavery less theoretical, more real. Harriet understood that once abolitionists heard her testimony, they were always both extremely sympathetic and more than willing to dole out financial support. The money Harriet raised from abolitionist circles was essential, but it too came with a cost. Each time she visited cities such as Boston, she put herself in immediate danger. Harriet may have been a powerful conductor on the Underground, but she was still a fugitive and could be apprehended anytime she left Canada. So even when she thought she was among like-minded people, Harriet relied on her wits to make sure she was truly with friends. For example, Harriet's illiteracy prevented her from reading notes of introduction, so to test new acquaintances, she always carried a small collection of cards with the faces of her abolitionist friends. If these new colleagues recognized their faces, she knew that she was safe.

Though it was dangerous, she could not avoid speaking to those interested in abolition. In addition to raising cash and resources that she could share with her family and the St. Catharines community, it raised awareness about the ways in which slavery was practiced. It also gave her access to men and women who would change her life for the better. Opportunities found their way to the newest anti-slavery star. It seemed everyone in abolitionist circles wanted to be Harriet's friend, or at the very least, claim her as an acquaintance. She was accustomed to navigating through marshland and the woods, but this was a new environment for Harriet, one that she mastered with the same fearlessness.

HOMEOWNER

Among her many fans was Senator William Seward. His proposition of 1859 was utterly unexpected. The New York senator was not a new friend; in fact, Harriet had known the antislavery governor, now senator, for some time. He and his wife, Frances, were known allies among the fugitive community. Nevertheless, when Seward approached Harriet with a real-estate proposition, she must have been stunned. The senator had inherited a farm from his father-in-law in the small town of Auburn, New York, and he wanted to give it to Harriet. This farming community in upstate New York had a dedicated cohort of antislavery activists who hid and supported fugitives on their way to Canada. Seward offered the seven-acre farm on South Street to Harriet for $1,200, an extremely reasonable price for the extensive property. A wooden home, a barn, and several other buildings accompanied the farmland that Harriet would call her own.

There was no way that Harriet could come up with $1,200 to purchase the property, but Seward allowed her to mortgage the house with extremely flexible payments. With a twenty-five-dollar down payment and a promise to make ten-dollar quarterly payments, Tubman was finally a homeowner. This was no small accomplishment for a fugitive black woman in the 1850s. She was neither considered free, nor was she considered a citizen, but she was a landowner, and with that came some semblance of security.

For Harriet's parents, the purchase of the home in Auburn was the news they hoped to hear. Ben and Rit Stewart had grown tired of St. Catharines, and Rit made it clear that Canadian winters were too difficult for her aged body. The Stewarts were not fugitives, so moving back to the United States would not be a risky venture. They could live out their days on their daughter's farm and benefit from the support of local antislavery allies. As she had done two years before, Harriet took care of her parents, even when it put her life in great danger. While her parents could cross the border without a problem, Harriet was still a fugitive and could never feel at ease in her own home.

Once her parents moved into the home on South Street, Harriet headed back to Boston to continue with her speaking engagements and earning as much money as possible. The mortgage wasn't, after all, going to pay itself.

THE GENERAL

Harriet's network of antislavery agitators stationed across the country was extensive, but she also developed a vital relationship with one of the most infamous abolitionists of the era. Harriet's bravery and knowledge of the Maryland terrain caught the attention of a man who was willing to stop at nothing to end the trade of human beings. John Brown would eventually lose his life in the fight to end slavery, but before that day came, he met and became friendly with the woman he would call "General."

Brown was born in Connecticut but spent a good deal of his life on the Ohio frontier, struggling to raise a family and move beyond poverty's reach. By the mid-1830s,

Brown was disillusioned with life but captivated by the abolitionist crusade. He became a radical antislavery agitator with a fervent belief that slavery needed to end immediately and by any means necessary. Unlike other abolitionists who believed in slow and nonviolent protest, John Brown was prepared to fight, maim, and kill those who stood in the way of his mission. In 1856, he moved to Kansas and joined the sectional battle to make Kansas a free state, using violence as a weapon against proslavery settlers. The guerilla warfare tactics he employed in this conflict were as violent as slavery itself. John Brown earned a reputation—he was not one to be dismissed.

With each passing year, Brown became more and more dissatisfied with the slow pace of slavery's demise. Frustrated and furious, he began to piece together a plan. He would build an army of abolitionists who would invade the South and convince enslaved men and women they met along the way to join their ranks. It would be a revolution—a revolution that would install a new government with a new constitution. Brown spent several weeks in Rochester, New York, at the home of Frederick Douglass, talking and thinking about his constitution and his future plans. The renegade abolitionist wanted the powerful orator and famous antislavery agitator to join his insurrection, but Frederick Douglass thought Brown's plans were foolish and would never successfully upend the power of the United States military. There was, however, another antislavery warrior that Brown wanted desperately to meet and recruit. He had heard about a woman who was known for her actions, not words, just the kind of person Brown needed in his army. In April of 1858, John Brown finally met the famous Harriet Tubman.

The first meeting between Brown and Tubman pumped new energy into his plan for insurrection. Because many abolitionists were uncomfortable with the idea of violence, Brown received tepid support from headliner activists. Most of them had never experienced slavery's cruelty and couldn't imagine joining or even supporting what appeared to be a fool's errand that would end in bloodshed. But Tubman was different. Like her associate Frederick Douglass, she knew slavery's violence all too well and had also grown tired of waiting for a peaceful end to it. By the late 1850s, most black people, especially fugitives, knew that slavery would never end without a fight. Only a war would end human bondage, and Harriet decided to throw her support behind the man who was not afraid to speak of the inevitable. It must have been refreshing to finally meet someone who had a concrete plan to end slavery. The trips back and forth from Maryland to Philadelphia and then Canada grew more difficult with each passing year, and even though she rescued nearly seventy people from slavery, Harriet understood this was a drop in the bucket. There were more than four million enslaved people across the nation, and she knew that one or two trips a year to the Eastern Shore only helped her family and friends. John Brown presented a plan that was risky and unlikely to succeed, but at least it was action, and this spoke to Harriet.

Armed rebellion against the United States would be almost impossible to plan, but Harriet's knowledge of allies and friends throughout Maryland could lend support to an attack in neighboring Virginia. More important, she agreed to use her influence among her friends in Canada to try to convince able-bodied men to join in Brown's future attack. If anyone could convince black men to leave the safety of Canada and engage in armed combat, it was Harriet. She had just as much to lose as the men she tried to recruit.

Brown paid Harriet twenty-five dollars in gold to support her recruitment efforts throughout the spring and summer. She traveled to Auburn, New York, in the fall to check in with her family, and then to Boston during the winter where, once again, she met up with John Brown. Harriet's support for Brown grew stronger, and she used her energy to raise funds for him during her speaking engagements across New England.

HARRIET'S HOMIES: FRIENDS AND ACQUAINTENCES

LUCRETIA MOTT

Abolitionist, pacifist, social reformer, and feminist activist who helped launch the women's rights movement

WILLIAM WELLS BROWN

Prominent abolitionist, journalist, lecturer, novelist, playwright, and historian

SOJOURNER TRUTH

Abolitionist, evangelist, and women's rights activist

JOHN BROWN

Fierce abolitionist and leader of the infamous 1859 raid on the federal arsenal at Harpers Ferry

FRANCES ELLEN WATKINS HARPER

Famed poet, abolitionist, suffragist, educator, orator, and writer

SUSAN B. ANTHONY

Abolitionist, social reformer, and women's rights activist

WILLIAM STILL

Conductor on the Underground Railroad, abolitionist, businessman, writer, historian, and civil rights activist

FREDERICK DOUGLASS

National leader in the abolitionist movement, social reformer, orator, writer, and statesman

ELIZABETH CADY STANTON

Abolitionist, human rights activist, suffragist, and one of the earliest leaders of the women's rights movement

WILLIAM LLOYD GARRISON

Outspoken abolitionist, journalist, suffragist, and social reformer

During a Fourth of July presentation, Harriet kept her audience spellbound and collected close to forty dollars—equal to twelve hundred dollars today—for her new comrade. As John Brown traveled down to Harpers Ferry, Virginia, where he planned to start his revolution, Harriet continued on her speaking tour, raising awareness and waiting for word about armed insurrection. On August 19, 1859, Brown made his last appeal to his friend Frederick Douglass, asking for his support in an attack against the arsenal at Harpers Ferry. The two met in Chambersburg, Pennsylvania, where he assured Douglass that enslaved men and women would throw down their tools and join in the rebellion once it began. Douglass disagreed and declined the invitation to fight, believing the strategy would be a certain failure.

Douglass was out, but Harriet remained a loyal supporter of Brown. During one of their earlier meetings, Harriet suggested that Brown begin the insurrection on Independence Day, an act that would send a symbolic message about freedom and democracy. But Brown was delayed, and revised details about the planned rebellion never found their way to Harriet's ears. When John Brown began his attack on October 16, 1859 at Harpers Ferry, he had only a small group of volunteer soldiers prepared to fight against the United States. Harriet was in New York at the time, and unaware that the battle had begun. Still, she had a bad feeling, perhaps a premonition, that something was terribly wrong. When Harriet eventually learned about the poor planning, the lack of support, and the bloody defeat that came so fast and furious, her intuition was confirmed.

By December 2, John Brown stood on the gallows, completely unapologetic about his actions, prepared to meet his maker. Harriet lost another ally to the power that supported slavery. If it wasn't clear before, Harriet knew that war was the only thing that could extinguish slavery's fire, but until that moment came, she vowed to chip away at the evil that kept so many in chains.

ONE LAST TIME

For nearly a decade, Harriet avoided capture as she went back into the lion's den to rescue friends and family. She never lost a fugitive to illness or capture, an accomplishment that reminded Harriet of her own strength and of God's power. Now in her late thirties, Harriet's body began to show the signs of ruthless wear and tear, making recovery from illness more and more difficult and prolonged. In addition to her rescue work, she had other stressors. With her new home, she carried a large financial responsibility that required her to tour across New England speaking out against slavery, work that was relentless and never secure.

With the federal crackdown following the raid on Harpers Ferry, many of Harriet's friends and family members advised her to return to Canada and to move about New England and upstate New York only when necessary and with the greatest of caution. Headstrong, Harriet didn't listen. There was one more dire mission to complete; she had to return to Maryland and try once again to rescue her sister Rachel and her two children, Angerine and Ben. With the exception of these three people, Harriet had pulled her entire immediate family that remained in Maryland away from slavery's hold. The thought of her sister languishing on the farm without any family support must have been torturous, not only for Harriet but also for her parents and brothers. Harriet was compelled to make one last trip to Dorchester County to rescue the last of her family members.

Just as she had done in the past, Harriet began the work of collecting funds for what was certain to be a dangerous trip. Dangerous because although eleven years had passed since she first escaped from Maryland, there was still a bounty on her head ranging upward of $12,000. Also, it was increasingly difficult for Harriet to keep a low profile; she was now a famous woman among antislavery circles, and her notoriety was a liability. On occasion, she would use pseudonyms, and the most famous abolitionist newspaper, *The Liberator*, referred to her simply as a "colored woman of the name Moses." But even these precautions were not fail-safe. Nonetheless, throughout the summer of 1860, she continued with speaking engagements across New England, collaborating with antislavery societies and abolitionists.

Despite her intense efforts, by the end of the summer, Harriet realized that she was still too short on cash to fund this last rescue and reached out to her friend and famed abolitionist Wendell Phillips. She asked him to make good on an earlier promise to assist her and to send money to a mutual friend in Philadelphia who would make certain it would find its way to Harriet. We don't know if she ever received the money.

With or without the necessary funding, she would press forward. Political events in the country left her no choice. As autumn of 1860 approached, the axis of the nation appeared to shift during a messy presidential election season and the South's mounting and heated response to Lincoln's candidacy.

Harriet quietly slipped into Dorchester County, Maryland, to rescue her loved ones. She knew this might be the last opportunity to free her remaining family members from bondage before the nation split in two. With a deep sense of urgency, Harriet stuck to the byways and the roads that she knew by heart and arrived safely on the Eastern Shore. When she arrived, her heart almost shattered. Shortly before Harriet reached the Eastern Shore, Rachel died, leaving her children separated on different farms without a parent. The details regarding Rachel's death are unknown, but the fact that the logistics didn't come together in time to save her sister must have been a wound Harriet lived with for the rest of her days. Too late to help Rachel, she now turned her attention to Angerine and Ben and to devising a rescue plan for the children.

When the time came, Harriet went to an agreed upon location to meet the children. She waited and waited for them, and even spent the night in the woods, constantly surveying her surroundings, praying to see the shadows of the two remaining family members. A November snowstorm blanketed the Eastern Shore of Maryland that night, leaving Harriet alone and in the cold. She took shelter behind a tree, but still the blinding snow and raging wind pummeled her small frame. Warrior that she was, she ignored the bone-chilling temperatures and the accumulating snow. But when morning came, Angerine and Ben were nowhere in sight. Harriet knew that slave-patrollers would soon resume their work. She had to leave the children behind. This, one of her few failures, could be attributed to lack of funds. Whether she was short of enough money to convince an accomplice to assist her, or to pay a watchful overseer to momentarily turn his back, or reasons we cannot fathom, the lack of money proved to be an insurmountable obstacle. True to form, she made certain that her trip was not in vain by whisking away a small group of runaways, including the Ennals family. They reached Delaware by the first of December, and while it took a bit more time than usual, they finally arrived in Canada by the end of the month. The runaways would celebrate New Year's Day of 1861 as free people but in Harriet's eyes, the mission was a failure.

Her last escape mission left Harriet exhausted and in dire need of recuperation. She traveled back to upstate New York to rest and tend to her frost-bitten feet, but her stay was brief as slave-catchers were spotted in and around the Auburn area. Their presence was a reminder of the intense sectarian crisis that had spun out of control and fractured the nation. While Harriet was busy on her last trip to Maryland, Abraham Lincoln was elected president of the United States, an event that prompted a furious response from Southern states. The Kentucky-born lawyer won the election of 1860 with only 40 percent of the popular vote, sending Southern Democrats into a tailspin. Even though the Supreme Court had ruled in their favor by protecting slavery, Southern states saw Lincoln's victory as a threat to their existence and immediately began to discuss plans for secession. Just five short weeks after Lincoln's election, the state of South Carolina seceded from the Union. It was quickly joined by six other states in the black belt of slave country. Mississippi, Alabama, Georgia, Louisiana, Florida, and Texas would shoulder up with South Carolina, forming the Confederate States of America, a new country that would continue the tradition of Southern life and custom without the interference of Northern imposition. Eventually, Virginia, Arkansas, Tennessee, and North Carolina would join this new confederacy.

During the spring of 1861, Harriet continued giving antislavery talks and attending abolitionist meetings in New England. The funds she collected from her events went to support the fugitive community in Canada and her family, but resources were harder than ever to come by as the nation prepared for armed combat. Harriet formalized her support for her runaway friends by organizing the Fugitive Aid Society of St. Catharines. Its goal was to offer financial support to fugitives who found their way to Canada. Her years on the antislavery circuit must have convinced Harriet that the best way to cultivate donors and supporters was to create a stable and staffed organization. The Fugitive Aid Society was run by Harriet's trusted family and friends, most of whom had fled from Delaware and Maryland. Their leadership was a symbol of the power and promise of formerly enslaved people.

MY PEOPLE ARE FREE

Several members of Harriet's family relocated from Canada and came to live in her New York home, so Harriet split her time between her community in St. Catharines and her family in Auburn. Money was always scarce, but Harriet's hard work and support from friends made certain that basic needs were met.

Times were tough, but for one moment in April of 1861, everyone's attention turned toward Fort Sumter in the Charleston Harbor. South Carolina had already seceded from the Union, and for months, they argued with federal officials over the military fort in their state. Only one month into his presidency, Lincoln had to confront the first military action of the Civil War; South Carolina's state militia bombarded Fort Sumter in a blatant show of military might and aggression against the United States of America. After thirty-four hours, Union forces had no choice but to surrender.

The sting of defeat turned quickly into a rallying cry for Northern citizens. Lincoln issued a call for volunteers, and optimism spread like wildfire across the Northern states. Tens of thousands of men volunteered for the Union Army, though black men were not initially allowed to enlist, a strategy Lincoln would have to revisit as the war dragged on.

Harriet knew that war would come to pass. She prophesized about the day of reckoning before the first shots rang through the air in South Carolina. Harriet told black abolitionist Henry Highland Garnet about her vision, but he dismissed her pessimistically. Garnet hoped that one day his grandchildren would witness the end of slavery, but he never believed that he would live to see national emancipation. Harriet disagreed with Garnet, telling him, *"You'll see it, and you'll see it soon. My people are free! My people are free!"* Her God had showed her that the war would end human bondage, and this vision coaxed the famous leader of fugitives to think seriously about her own role in the war for independence.

PART III
BAWSS LADY

WAR ZONE

By the fall of 1861, six months into the war, Americans realized that there would be nothing short or bloodless about this conflict. Casualties were mounting and the need for volunteer Union soldiers and supplies grew with each passing month. Northerners, especially abolitionists, came together to donate money, sew blankets, and collect supplies to send to the Union troops stationed in places like South Carolina and Virginia. Harriet heard reports about the tough conditions for Union soldiers, reports that generated more donations and sympathy. As soon as the Union army set up their command posts in towns across the Confederacy, enslaved men and women ran from their owners looking for asylum with the men dressed in blue. They weren't always met with kindness. Indeed, reports about the terrible conditions and mistreatment of former slaves weighed heavily on Harriet's heart.

Across Hilton Head Island, St. Helena Island, and Beaufort, South Carolina, the enslaved took shelter in the military zone established by Union forces and soon became known as contraband. One Union general declared that all of the enslaved who made their way to his camp were free, but President Lincoln quickly reversed that decision. His stance on slavery was still ambiguous, and for Lincoln, this was a war to reunite the nation, not to free the nearly four million black people still in bondage. Lincoln was in no hurry to push states like Maryland and Delaware to join the Confederacy and he worried that if he appeared too eager to emancipate the enslaved, his actions might drive other border states into the arms of the enemy. Lincoln refused to even allow black men the right to fight for the Union Army until 1862, and only when a dire need for additional manpower made it necessary.

None of this sat well with Harriet. For more than a decade, she had been in the business of emancipating people, and the new president appeared hesitant to follow suit. Lincoln made no promises about emancipating anyone, and instead was interested in solving the problem of slavery by colonizing black people in faraway lands. Lincoln believed that resettling emancipated black men and women to Central America or the continent of Africa was the best way to solve the problem of slavery and the racial divide. Congress supported the president and allocated $100,000 to support colonization. Harriet knew what it meant to be banished to another country and had no intention of relocating to Panama or Liberia. She was troubled by her president's actions, but she remembered the visions that came to her in one of her dream states, visions that promised freedom. Harriet knew that emancipation was coming, no matter what Lincoln said or did. Still, she was never one to sit around and wait for things to happen. She began to think about how she could get directly involved to help ensure the end of slavery. Just as she was calculating what her next steps would be, the governor of Massachusetts, John Andrew, contacted her. He had a favor to ask of Harriet.

Activists across New England knew that they had to unleash every powerful weapon in their arsenal to fight the Confederacy, and they knew of one person who had a proven track record of success in outmaneuvering Southerners; that was Harriet Tubman. Through her many abolitionist friends, Harriet was introduced to John Andrew, a former lawyer who offered legal support to John Brown following the raid on Harpers Ferry. Aware of her reputation and successful track record, the governor recognized that Harriet's many talents could be put to good use in the fight against the Confederacy. Harriet's intimate knowledge of the marshlands on the Eastern Shore of Maryland could come in handy for the Union officers stationed on the swampy shores of South Carolina. She was already a proven scout with an uncanny ability to remain hidden in plain sight, making the governor's decision an easy one. Harriet was perfectly suited to be a spy for the Union Army, if she only agreed to do so. The governor asked her to sail down to Beaufort, South Carolina, and put her many talents to good use, because he believed "she would be a valuable person to operate within the enemies [sic] lines in procuring information and scouts." Harriet didn't need convincing. For her, not only was this an opportunity to help secure a Union victory, it was also an opportunity to help former slaves begin anew.

For the first time in her life, Harriet traveled to the Deep South, arriving in Beaufort sometime in the spring of 1862. She was still technically a fugitive, and Harriet knew what could happen if she was captured by Confederate troops. At the very least, she would be reenslaved, or worse yet, die a slow and horrible death at the hands of angry slaveholders aware of her notable identity and formidable past. After all, in liberating her kin and others, she had decreased the value of the estates of their owners. If captured, she was likely to come to a horrendous end. If she was fearful, it never showed.

Though riskier than ever, given her status, Harriet arrived safely in South Carolina and immediately realized that she had walked into the middle of a social experiment. Union troops had invaded the Port Royal Sound in November of 1861 and successfully taken control of the Sea Islands. They watched as slaveholders fled their properties, leaving behind nearly ten thousand enslaved men, women, and children, who would begin their lives as free people on the plantations they knew well. They worked the land of their former owners as wage laborers and sold their surplus crops at market. This "Port Royal Experiment" would prove, the organizers hoped, that if exposed to education and structured freedom, black men and women would and could live as honest and hardworking people.

The questioning of black intentions must have sounded foolish to Harriet. Her family and friends were proof of just how ridiculous it was to doubt black progress with the absence of slavery. Harriet's own life refuted this fallacy. She owned a home, had founded a mutual aid organization, and took care of her family and friends. No one had to teach her how to be a productive member of society, and the very questioning of black ability and integrity must have rubbed Harriet the wrong way.

Originally tasked with the work of espionage, Harriet instead found herself shuttled into assisting the troops by handing out much-needed Northern donations. This was not the work that Harriet was originally called to do. She wasn't capturing and sharing information about the enemy. Demoted because of her race and gender, she was tasked with domestic duties rather than intelligence-gathering. This was probably not surprising for the fugitive-turned-military-advisor. As a black woman, with those two strikes against her, she had experienced bigotry before. She accepted the demotion and soldiered on.

She wanted to spend her days scouting or helping former slaves, but her service for the Christian Commission was a priority in the minds of the Union leadership. Harriet later recalled, *"I first took charge of the Christian Commission house at Beaufort,"* an operation established by the YMCA to distribute clothing, blankets, food, and books to Union Soldiers.

Eventually, Harriet got closer to the action—perhaps it was her name recognition that gave Harriet a little flexibility with her assignments, or maybe she negotiated with the men in charge of her detail. Harriet was finally assigned to help the black men and women living around the Union camps. Although it had been almost thirteen years since she first escaped from Maryland, she remembered the gnawing hunger and the physical pain from her time in bondage. Harriet didn't know the former slaves in Beaufort, but she could connect to them and their experiences; they were her brothers and sisters.

Runaways who fled from plantations and farms arrived at Union camps with nothing, only the set of ragged clothes that they wore day in and day out. Harriet watched as thousands poured into the camp, looking for safety and the promise of freedom, but instead were met with chaos and frustration. No one knew how long the war would last, but Harriet knew this: the Union army would not become the caretaker for their so-called contraband. Former slaves had to find a way to take care of themselves. Harriet received a $200 grant from the government to set up a "wash house" where the freedwomen could earn a little money by washing the clothing of Union soldiers. Freedwomen gathered together to perform other work like sewing and cooking, skills they had perfected, and which were desperately needed in the campgrounds. With meager rations, Union soldiers always complained about hunger, so they looked to freedwomen to turn their foraged wild pigs and sheep into freshly cooked dinners.

Harriet watched black women struggle to provide for themselves and began to feel uncomfortable with her advantages. As a recruit, she was given rations like the other soldiers, but her privilege did not sit well with freedmen and freedwomen in Beaufort, and this made her uncomfortable. The last thing she wanted to do was to cause friction in her new community, so she decided to forgo what meager rations she was due. To make ends meet, Harriet joined the other freedwomen and started selling pies and root beer to hungry soldiers. Aside from her humility, Harriet remembered that she was called to South Carolina to do intelligence work, and to be effective at that job, the last thing she needed was to be known and resented by the former slaves. Should she ever get a chance to work as a spy, as she was recruited to do, she would have to rely upon her new friends for their knowledge, their connections, and any valuable information that could help in her generating intelligence. Harriet needed to do more than blend in, she needed to be respected and trusted.

SICK AND TIRED

She gained this trust by performing some of the most important work among the soldiers and the freedmen: she was drafted to nurse the sick and console the dying. Harriet was assigned to work with Dr. Henry K. Durant, a physician and medical director of the freedmen's hospital at Port Royal, where she witnessed unimaginable suffering. More men would die of disease than bullets during the war, as yellow fever and cholera turned healthy men into mere shadows of themselves. Dysentery wreaked havoc on the intestines of men who languished in unsanitary conditions, as flies, feces, and food carried germs that wiped out entire regiments and caused devastation among the civilian population.

There were only a handful of available medications that treated diseases, so the sick depended upon botanical concoctions. Harriet would have collected blackberries and brewed chamomile tea to soothe inflamed bowels. She also remembered that paregoric, which she used to drug fugitive babies, served as an antidiarrheal. Appreciated for her knowledge of herbal remedies, Harriet continued to gain the trust and admiration of the freedmen and freedwomen around the camp. Among the formerly enslaved, her knowledge carried more weight than the advice of Dr. Durant. She was well known for her Underground leadership, but in the camps, she became legendary for her medical care.

Tubman, a Union Nurse Caring for the Sick and Dying

Once again, her race and gender got in the way of proper recognition. Even though she saved lives and nursed dying men back to life, she never received compensation for this new assignment, relying upon her own entrepreneurship to support herself and provide money to send to her family in New York. In addition to the "wash house," Harriet opened an "eating house" for freedmen and officers alike. In order to bake her pies and gingerbread, she scoured the docks by Beaufort's wharf, looking for the best prices for flour, sugar, and salt. She haggled with farmers and storeowners who took advantage of wartime shortages. Basic ingredients were in short supply and high demand.

Harriet sold her baked goods for cash and hired freedmen to sell her food throughout the camps. Just to turn a profit, Harriet would work through the night, baking upward of fifty pies an evening, producing large quantities of gingerbread, and brewing two casks of root beer. In the little time there was to rest, Harriet made her way to the Savan House, where she took up residence. While nursing the sick by day and baking goods at night, Harriet was intentional about her unspoken mission: she was constantly gathering information about everything and everyone. The freedmen who grew to respect Harriet whispered delicate information about Confederate whereabouts in the most subtle of conversations. The men she nursed back to health and the women she taught how to launder clothes made certain to share everything they understood with their new leader. Harriet knew where the men in gray stationed themselves, how low they ran on rations, and what their next plan of action might be. Once she gathered the intelligence, she shared it with Generals Hunter and Sherman, and Colonel Montgomery, high-ranking men who accepted her information with appreciation. Harriet proved herself capable of doing the job she was originally asked to do, and in a short time, she was asked to begin scouting for the Union army.

BLACK MOSES

She moved about in disguise—sometimes as a poor farm wife or an unnoticed field hand—infiltrating Confederate strongholds and gathering vital intelligence. Harriet slipped in and out of enemy territory, listening and watching closely, eventually returning to repeat many things the Union officers were glad to know. Dribs and drabs of intelligence helped slow the Confederate pace, but Union leaders wanted a definitive win, which entailed finally assigning Harriet to formally gather intelligence. She was assigned a mission on the Combahee River, a short waterway that emptied into St. Helena Sound near Beaufort. As Colonel James Montgomery was one of John Brown's men, Harriet felt comfortable working with him, and in the end became more of a partner than an advisor.

Harriet put together a team of trusted local freedmen—former slaves who knew the waterways and the winding coastal lowlands better than any Northern Union soldier. Her party set out to scan the Combahee River, knowing it was a booby trap that the Confederates had littered with naval mines. Southern soldiers wanted nothing more than to see Union rivercraft explode into pieces, maiming and killing each and every soldier onboard. Harriet's crew reached out to the men and women who were still enslaved and living behind Confederate lines. They spoke in whispers and learned the precise locations of the naval bombs. Once Harriet's team carefully collected their information, they were ready to proceed.

Confident with their intelligence gathering and under the cover of darkness, Colonel Montgomery, Harriet, and close to three hundred black soldiers sailed slowly up the Combahee, intent on destroying Confederate territory. Their plan was to cut off the stream of supplies that fed and clothed Southern soldiers and to liberate as many enslaved people as their ship could carry. This was a rescue mission perfectly made for Harriet.

Shortly after sunrise on June 2, 1863, Harriet sailed silently up the river on a Union gunboat, avoiding the torpedoes that lay in wait. The darkness of night and the soundlessness of Harriet and her men caught sleeping Confederate soldiers by surprise. The thunder of gunboat shells and the image of black soldiers marching up the causeway temporarily stunned the soldiers in gray, and when they came to their senses it was simply too late. Harriet's men reached the shoreline, climbed off their boats, and tore through the grand plantations that housed the Confederates. Southern soldiers and slaveholders went fleeing into the woods while Harriet's men torched and pillaged homes, barns, and storehouses. Billowing black smoke and blistering heat irritated the eyes and lungs of Harriet's men, but they soldiered on, steadfast in their mission. They took pleasure in watching Southern symbols of slavery burn and fall to the ground. They succeeded in destroying everything in sight.

Passengers on the Savannah Railroad saw the blaze of burning property. For a fifteen-mile stretch, everything along the Combahee was cloaked in an orange glow. Black soldiers broke down floodgates, swallowing up rice fields that had been planted by the enslaved. Harriet watched as the pain and violence of rice cultivation were erased and replaced by the tranquility of newly formed lakes. The only thing left unscathed by roving soldiers were the slave quarters.

Enslaved men and women were on their way to the rice fields, prepared to spend another day working under the lash, when they realized that liberation had come their way. Thunderous gunboats rang out like a starter's pistol, prompting hundreds of slaves to drop their tools and run for the Union boats. Overseers tried in vain to restore order and obedience, relying on whips and pistols to beat and terrify their human property into submission. But their threats fell upon deaf ears. Ignoring the commands of her overseer, one enslaved girl ran toward the Union boats, but she wasn't fast enough to outrun her overseer's bullets. She fell to the ground. Mustering whatever strength was required, she rose up and joined the others who saw freedom within reach.

They ran down every road and across every field with the goal of climbing aboard a Union ship. Grabbing their babies and a few possessions, they headed for the river. With their bundles and baskets perched on hips, shoulders, and heads, they brought with them squealing pigs and screaming chickens, dodging Confederate gunshots and the snapping jaws of angry dogs. The number of fleeing people quickly swelled into the hundreds, and Harriet, for a moment, was overcome with righteous indignation and unadulterated joy. She and the soldiers doubled over in laughter as the enslaved continued to make their way onto Union gunboats. From the upper deck Harriet yelled out, "Come along! Come along!"—and in just a short time, Harriet's ship was loaded to capacity.

Close to 750 newly freed men and women sailed to Beaufort in a state of astonishment and relief. They didn't know what kind of future was in store for them, but anything was better than the threat of the lash. Their joy, however, was quickly tempered by the cries of those left behind. There simply wasn't enough room to carry everyone away. Harriet's happiness soon gave way to agony as she watched men and women on the shores from which they had departed racked with anguished grief. As her ship sailed down the Combahee, Harriet must have thought about her sisters Linah, Mariah Ritty, and Soph, who had also been left behind, swallowed up by the slavery of the Deep South.

In Beaufort, a boisterous Colonel Montgomery offered his congratulations and asked the woman who had organized the raid to address the crowd. In front of her stood soldiers and hundreds of newly freed men and women who wanted nothing more than to hear from their leader, the black woman who outmaneuvered the Confederates and ushered hundreds to freedom. While we don't know the exact words she offered, she most likely began her speech with a prayer of thanks to God before congratulating her soldiers and welcoming them to the opportunities that came with freedom. Perhaps she consoled those who left family and loved ones on the shores of the Combahee River, telling them about her prophecy that freedom would eventually find its way to everyone. Her words were met with shouts of celebration and optimism, a feeling that the freedmen had rarely, if ever, experienced. A reporter from the *Wisconsin State Journal* who witnessed the events in South Carolina reported on everything he saw that day. He called Harriet "A Black She Moses."

Harriet's raid on the Combahee dealt a devastating blow to the Confederacy. Causing nearly two million dollars in property damage and the loss of hundreds of slaves, Harriet became the first woman, black or white, to plan and lead an armed military expedition during the Civil War. Her strategy supported a form of combat new to the Civil War—a type of "scorched earth" warfare that left nothing to chance. In Harriet's mind, everything about slavery needed to be destroyed, and she felt no pity over the loss of property or Confederate life. Having come face-to-face with their cruelty, she knew that Southern slaveholders would never voluntarily end human bondage; they would need to be cancelled out. Black troops stared into the faces of Confederate soldiers with a fierce preparedness, reminding everyone, from the cooks in the Union camps up to Abraham Lincoln, that they were more than able to fight. They were hungry for victory, and under Harriet's leadership, they would find it.

Tubman Joyful after Commanding a Military Raid

TO DIE WITH VALOR

She spent time with the newly freed men and women in Beaufort, trying to find jobs, food, and shelter for the new arrivals. Many of the men joined Colonel Montgomery's troop, but nonetheless, life remained difficult for former slaves. They would quickly learn that freedom was far from easy. In a month's time, Union forces moved to attack Charleston, and the regiments stationed in Beaufort traveled the seventy miles to join the fight. Harriet followed the soldiers to the Charleston Harbor, but once again, she served as a nurse and a cook. Harriet made no public complaints about this assignment, because she knew she was ill-prepared to spy on the Confederates in Charleston. She was in a position, however, to watch the famed all black Fifty-Fourth Massachusetts Regiment arrive at Fort Wagner under the leadership of Colonel Robert Gould Shaw. She even knew some of the men in this regiment, including the sons of her famous friend Frederick Douglass. Before the war, the former-fugitive-turned-abolitionist spoke out against slavery on the lecture circuit and in his autobiography. Once the war began, Douglass actively encouraged black recruitment. Lewis and Charles Douglass joined the army with the full support of their father, and along with the other men in the regiment, they prepared for some of the fiercest fighting seen in the war. Before the men left for battle, Harriet prepared breakfast for Colonel Shaw. It would be his last meal.

On July 18, 1863, the Fifty-Fourth Massachusetts Volunteer Infantry spearheaded the assault on Fort Wagner. They rushed toward the thirty-foot walls that surrounded the fort, running directly into a barrage of bullets and brutal hand-to-hand combat. The raid was a disaster. No one imagined the Union loses would be so great. Nearly six hundred men died, went missing, or were captured, while Confederate losses were minor. Harriet's friends and acquaintances in the Fifty-Fourth were decimated. Close to 40 percent of the black soldiers died on the beaches in

Shaw's nurse at memorial (Boston Herald, *May 31, 1905*).

front of Fort Wagner. She would later poetically describe the carnage she witnessed: *"And when we saw the lightning, and that was the guns; and when we heard the thunder, and that was the big guns; and then we heard the rain falling, and that was the drops of blood falling; and when we came to get the crops, it was the dead we reaped."*

Harriet rushed back to Beaufort to tend to the sick. Men arrived with missing limbs and burned bodies—deafened and blinded from bomb blasts. Black soldiers took shelter at the hospital, where Harriet met them with what little medicine there was available. She took care of them the best she could, but squalid conditions made healing almost impossible. Later in her life, Harriet recalled just how terrible the conditions were for her soldiers:

> *I'd go to the hospital, I would, early every morning. I'd get a big chunk of ice, I would, and put it in a basin, and fill it with water; then I'd take a sponge and begin. First man I'd come to, I'd thrash away the flies, and they'd arise, they would, like bees round a hive. Then I'd begin to bathe their wounds, and by the time I'd bathed off three or four, the fire and heat would have melted the ice and made the water warm, and it would be as red as clear blood. Then I'd go and get more ice, I would, and by the time I got to the next ones, the flies would be round de first ones, black and thick as ever.*

As she continued to nurse the sick during the day and bake pies at night, she couldn't help but worry about her parents. She dictated a letter to her journalist and reformer friend Franklin Benjamin Sanborn, in which she revealed her concerns: *"I have now been absent two years almost, and have just got letters from my friends in Auburn, urging me to come home. My father and mother are old and in feeble health and need my care and attention."*

Her skills were needed in South Carolina even more, however, as the stream of sick and dying men continued to pour into the hospital. It wasn't until the fall of 1863 that Harriet received leave to return to New York. Once she saw that her parents were well, she took a trip to Canada to check in on her brother William Henry and on the community of fugitives in St. Catharines. Although Lincoln's Emancipation Proclamation took effect earlier that year, it only offered freedom to the enslaved living in Confederate states. The Proclamation did nothing for those who lived in border states like Maryland, Delaware, Missouri, Kentucky, and West Virginia. Because these states never declared an allegiance with the Confederacy, Lincoln allowed them to keep their slaves. Harriet and her friends and family remained the legal property of their Maryland owners. This indignity must have infuriated

William Henry [Ross] Stewart, one of Harriet Tubman's brothers who fled to Canada. Photo probably taken in Canada circa 1860.

the proven scout, spy, nurse, baker, and cook. Harriet was good enough to lend her service to the Union Army but was never emancipated by Abraham Lincoln. She would have to remind herself that she was fighting a war to end slavery, not a war to serve the president of the United States. This would be the only reason she'd agree to return to South Carolina and travel to Jacksonville, Florida, in early 1864.

Harriet continued to tend to sick soldiers for another six months, but her patience with the ways in which black soldiers—herself included—were treated began to wear thin. She took deep offense each time she witnessed subpar treatment handed down to black soldiers. For example, they received less than half the pay of white soldiers. Even Harriet, while in service, never received compensation for her nursing duties.

FURLOUGH

By June of 1864, Harriet was ready to leave the South, and was given a furlough to travel to New York City and then to Boston. She met with her abolitionist friends and was introduced to another black woman activist, Sojourner Truth. Born Isabella Baumfree in New York, Truth shared a few things in common with Harriet. She too had been enslaved and had fled from bondage, eventually becoming an abolitionist and later on, an activist for women's rights. The two women talked politics, but Harriet was less than convinced by Truth's favorable opinion of their president. Unlike Sojourner Truth, Harriet was still not a free woman.

During her travels in New England, Harriet's health took a turn for the worse, which forced her to tend to her own exhausted body and overstay her furlough. When she had regained her health and attempted to return to her wartime duties, she was denied transportation and had to wait another month before she was granted permission from the War Department to travel to Hilton Head, South Carolina. While she waited for her transport vessel, Harriet made a quick trip to Philadelphia where she visited with the Twenty-Fourth United States Colored Troops, sharing her stories about her time in the South. Harriet had no idea that this trip would change her future plans.

HARRIET BY THE NUMBERS

BIRTH:
1822

SIBLINGS: 8

HUSBANDS: 2

DEATH:
3|10|1913

YEAR SHE ESCAPED:
1849

STATES CROSSED: 8

FOLKS CARRIED TO FREEDOM FROM MARYLAND:

TRIPS ON THE UNDERGROUND RAILROAD: 13

60–70

DECLARATION OF HARRIET ON THE $20 BILL BY THE OBAMA ADMINISTRATION: 4|20|2016

Sojourner Truth, 1864.

Right before her departure from Philadelphia, Harriet was approached by a group of nurses from the United States Sanitary Commission. They suggested that Harriet forgo her trip to South Carolina and instead, travel with them to Virginia and work in some of the hospitals along the James River. Harriet jumped at the opportunity—an indication that she was far from excited about returning to South Carolina. Once she arrived at Fort Monroe in Hampton, Virginia, Harriet continued to comfort and hold the hands of dying black soldiers.

For three years, Harriet had served the Union army in multiple ways, but by April of 1865, everything had changed. Confederate general Robert E. Lee surrendered and five days later, Abraham Lincoln was assassinated. The war was over and Harriet's lifelong dream finally came to pass. The Thirteenth Amendment to the Constitution prohibited slavery, emancipating nearly four million people of African descent. We don't know how Harriet celebrated the news of a Union victory or how she reacted to universal freedom. A devout Christian,

Harriet probably dropped to her knees and thanked God for keeping his promise, and then she may have asked for strength and guidance. Although freedom had come, Harriet knew that racism and bigotry would not evaporate overnight; in fact, like most black people, she assumed that she would have to fight against oppression for the rest of her life. Time would prove Harriet right.

PART IV
CALL ME MRS. DAVIS

Harriet Tubman,
between circa 1871–1876.

A WAR HERO

The war was over, but Harriet's work was not. As a nurse at the colored hospital at Fort Monroe, she continued to watch black soldiers languish in horrible conditions, an injustice that Harriet couldn't dismiss. The end of the war made her question the inequities around her and push for the next logical step—citizenship and equal treatment. Tired of the neglect, she traveled to Washington, DC, in the summer of 1865 to complain about the atrocious conditions suffered by black soldiers. She confronted the surgeon general, informing him that black soldiers died at an astonishing rate—two and a half times that of white soldiers. For weeks, Harriet continued to lobby anyone and everyone she knew in positions of power and pressed for progress, for her men and for herself. It soon became painfully clear, however, that the freedom gained by the Civil War would not translate to fair and equal treatment.

Harriet's frustrations continued to mount. In addition to her anger over the treatment of black soldiers, she grew tired of being penniless. She took an account of her work and service for the military and grew resentful. For three and a half years she had cared for sick soldiers and put her life in danger—and had only received $200. In her mind, the days of pie baking were over; it was time to be compensated. Before leaving Washington, DC, she approached her friend, Secretary of State William Seward, with another request—an urgent need of her own. She asked

Seward to help her apply to the government for back pay and he agreed to look into it for her. Harriet left Washington, DC, with a twelve-dollar loan from Seward and a tepid promise of assistance.

Surgeon General Joseph K. Barnes appointed Harriet as nurse or matron at the colored hospital in Virginia, but when she arrived at Fort Monroe, her promised assignment had disappeared. Harriet had no intentions of continuing in an unpaid nursing position. She knew she deserved more. So she made the decision to walk away from her injured and dying men. No longer was she needed as a scout or a spy, and there were other women who could fill her nursing shoes. The war was over, and Harriet needed to find a new mission in life. As ever, her family in New York and Canada was calling to her. Like millions of others, Harriet would have to figure out what it meant to live in a nation where black people were free but still cemented to poverty and poor treatment.

NORTHERN REALITIES

On her way home to New York in October of 1865, Harriet stopped for a visit outside of Philadelphia with famed women's-rights leader Lucretia Mott. Harriet knew that Mott was still mourning the loss of her daughter, and she wanted to pay her respects. They talked about many things during their visit, probably discussing Harriet's time and her service for the Union and the hot-button political topic of black-male suffrage. It would have been a strange meeting if the two didn't talk about women's rights and the need to fight for universal suffrage. Eventually, Harriet said goodbye to her friend and boarded a train from Philadelphia to New York with a "half-fare ticket"—a benefit given to veterans for their service. She immediately encountered resistance. The conductor refused to accept Harriet's ticket, telling her to move to the smoker, the car located directly behind the locomotive that spewed black smoke and soot on top of its passengers. Tired of poor treatment and empty promises, Harriet decided she wasn't moving and informed the conductor that she worked for the government and could stay exactly where she was seated. Infuriated, the conductor decided to take matters into his own hands by attempting to physically remove Harriet; he had no idea with whom he was messing.

Harriet's small frame was deceiving, and it took a few moments before the conductor realized that he was in for a fight. Harriet must have sized him up and knew that if he put his hands on her she could take him down. Maybe she didn't expect physical violence from a white man in Philadelphia after the war, but the dividing line between North and South was blurry when it came to black equality. The two struggled, and Harriet held on to the interior of the train compartment, refusing to lose ground. When the humiliated conductor realized that he was too weak to remove Harriet from the train car, his fury metastasized. Reinforcements appeared in the form of two additional train conductors, and the three of them grabbed Harriet, pulling her arm so hard that it broke. They threw her into the smoking car and injured her again, breaking several of her ribs.

Not one white bystander came to her aid. Most of them watched the assault, and a few even heckled and jeered, telling the lead conductor to throw Harriet off the train. While fighting off the conductors, she took note of the white people in the train car and realized that she would have to combat more than the three men on the train. These men represented the vast majority of white Northerners—the Americans who sided with the Union army. This was the North. These supposed countrymen for whom she had risked her life degraded and assaulted her, a lesson that she would never forget.

Harriet was injured but she would not be silenced. She called the conductor a *"copperhead scoundrel"* (a name hurled at Northern men and women who sympathized with the South) and reminded him that *"she didn't thank anybody to call her a colored person—She would be called black or Negro—she was as proud of being a black woman as he was of being white."* Harriet did not have the strength to fight off three men, but she found power in her voice. Many knew her as a woman of action, but now Harriet would need to change course. There were no longer fugitives to lead to safety or Confederate troops to defeat. Instead, there was a prejudice against her race and gender that required a new strategy for its destruction. Harriet would be reminded that her words had power.

THE KINDNESS OF STRANGERS

The train ride back to New York was both a reminder of the difficulties that lay ahead and a harbinger of things to come. But for the moment, Harriet simply needed to rest, though the pressures of caring for a large family didn't allow the war hero much time to recuperate. She returned to a house that was teeming with people, not just her elderly parents, Ben and Rit, who needed attention. Harriet's niece Ann Stewart and her husband Thomas had moved into the home, as had Harriet's sister-in-law Catherine Stewart and her two children, Esther and Elijah, along with a boarder. Margaret Stewart, Harriet's "favorite niece," also lived with the family. All of the Ross/Stewart family knew that Harriet adored Margaret, evidenced by the special treatment she showered upon her—actions that sometimes caused friction among family members. For example, when Harriet prepared to leave for her assigned work in the Civil War, she sent Margaret to live with white patron Lazette Worden, sister of Frances Seward (the secretary of state's wife). Margaret was only ten years old when the war broke out, and for a handful of years, she was treated to an education and a finer standard of living than were her other family members. This didn't always sit well with Harriet's kinfolk.

In addition, there was a bit of mystery and some controversy surrounding Margaret's arrival in New York. She was born sometime around 1850 and remembered traveling to the North by steamship with her Aunt Harriet. Possibly the daughter of one of Harriet's brothers, Margaret was taken to New York and raised by Harriet, who treated her more like a daughter than a niece, insofar as her schedule allowed. Eventually however, Harriet's speaking engagements and her service to the Union made parenting almost impossible, so she leaned on her network of friends and family in Auburn to help raise Margaret in her absence. But later in life, Harriet was accused of taking Margaret out of Maryland without the permission of her free parents. These accusations were difficult to confirm and ran counter to all of Harriet's previous actions, but as the years wore on, a veil of mystery surrounding Margaret's arrival still lingered. No matter the circumstances of her arrival, Harriet and Margaret cared deeply for one another.

In a short time, Harriet's niece Kessiah Bowley and her family also took up temporary residence on South Street, and soon there was a constant stream of injured, orphaned, and destitute souls who showed up on Harriet's doorstep. She could never turn anyone away. Harriet thought about the many people who offered her reprieve and support while on her escape missions and bristled at the thought of turning her back on homeless, disabled, and hungry black people. She had very little to offer the needy, but she believed that God would always provide.

The injuries Harriet suffered when she was abused on the train left her unable to work for most of the fall and winter. Without her contribution, household supplies dwindled to nothing. Stomachs grumbled and winter coats wore thin. Thankfully, Harriet's friends made certain that the famed fugitive and her family didn't starve.

It must have been difficult for Harriet to ask for assistance. She was a woman accustomed to fixing problems by her own might, so to ask for money from her white abolitionist friends or a soup bone from a local butcher might have driven a leader like Harriet into depression or dysfunctional resentment. But Harriet saw herself as a servant leader, commissioned by God to help others. For the moment, her task was to provide for her family and those who needed her support, and she would do it by any means necessary. Harriet wasn't too proud to accept the kindness of strangers.

TALL, DARK, AND HANDSOME

In the midst of the difficulties and drudgery of everyday life, a welcome surprise appeared on Harriet's doorstep in Auburn. Private Nelson Charles was a young and handsome black veteran who likely made Harriet's acquaintance during the war years. He had been enslaved near Elizabeth City, North Carolina, but ran away to upstate New York sometime around 1861. He was nineteen years old when he joined the New York Eighth Regiment in 1863, and like nearly 180,000 other black soldiers, he risked his life for the Union cause. He trained at Camp William Penn, located just outside of Philadelphia, and was eventually deployed to South Carolina. Perhaps he met Harriet in Beaufort, or maybe their paths crossed in Jacksonville, Florida, or at Fort Monroe in Virginia. While we don't know the details about their first encounter, it must have been enough to make an honorably discharged soldier find his way from Brownsville, Texas, to Auburn, New York. Nelson Charles shed his slave name, began calling himself Nelson Davis, and took up residence as a boarder in Harriet's home. Like many black veterans, he was simply trying to build a new life by scraping by, eventually finding work as a brickmaker.

Harriet made room in her crowded house for the tall soldier. He was nearly twenty years younger than she, and he suffered from many of the illnesses that plagued Civil War veterans. Nelson had contracted one of the worst offenders—tuberculosis. Known as "consumption," the disease was deadly and could wipe out entire communities. We don't know when or where Nelson contracted the disease, but he probably first noticed a stubborn cough, one that prevented him from sound sleep. He would have detected that some of the other men in his regiment had a similar bone-rattling cough that simply never went away. As a formerly enslaved person, Nelson was familiar with fatigue, but for some reason, he simply couldn't shake his tiredness. It wasn't a fatigue that would disappear after a good night's sleep; it was constant and unrelenting, and his weight loss was dramatic. The night sweats would soak through his clothing and keep Nelson cold and damp as his cough worsened. If he covered his mouth while he coughed, he likely saw droplets of blood snake down the palm of his hand.

There was no cure for tuberculosis, nor was there any effective treatment. Doctors told their patients to rest, eat well, and spend time outdoors, but these recommendations saved no one. Most people didn't survive, but those who did lived with a constant reminder of their ailment. Nelson managed to beat the odds, but he would never be the same. When he arrived at Harriet's home she didn't worry about contagion; instead, she welcomed him to Auburn, and did what came naturally to her: she took care of him.

As Harriet helped Nelson get on his feet, news from Dorchester County, Maryland, found its way to Auburn. She learned that her first husband, John Tubman, was involved in a violent altercation with a white neighbor. A minor argument between two men resulted in devastating violence as the white neighbor drew his gun and fatally shot John Tubman in the forehead. Harriet's first husband died on September 30, 1867. The neighbor, Robert Vincent, was charged with murder and went to trial, but an all-white jury acquitted him in record speed. The black newspapers railed at the verdict, exposing the clear lack of justice handed down by a jury that consisted of Southern Democrats—the party of the Confederacy:

That Vincent murdered the deceased we presume no one doubts; but as no one but a colored boy saw him commit the deed, it was universally conceded that he would be acquitted, the moment it was ascertained that the jury was composed exclusively of Democrats.

Fifteen years had passed since Harriet had last encountered the man whom she deemed a cheat. Perhaps she had reconciled what she believed to be his abandonment of her, or maybe she still possessed feelings of resentment and anger. However Harriet processed the news of her first husband's murder, it was a reminder of just how dangerous it was for a black man to test his power in post–Civil War America.

• • •

Meanwhile, Harriet had more immediate and very serious concerns to tend to; she needed money. Never abandoning the idea that she was owed back pay for her service in the army, Harriet hoped that her appeal to her friend, Secretary of State William Seward, would eventually pay off. She waited patiently, hoping that good news would come, followed by a monthly war pension. She waited in vain.

In November of 1867, Harriet appealed to other friends, asking former abolitionist Gerrit Smith to scrounge up support to make a formal appeal for retroactive pay and a pension for her time as a scout, nurse, and spy. After her visit with Seward, Harriet began collecting documents, proof that she had actually been in South Carolina, Florida, and Virginia. Piecing together a fragmented wartime experience as an illiterate woman was difficult, but she did her best, and passed these documents along to her friends with name recognition.

Harriet and Her Second Husband, Nelson Davis

After looking over Harriet's documentation, suffragist and writer Sallie Holley took to the newspapers to tell the general public about the great injustice. Harriet's denied request and her recent difficulties appeared in *The National Anti-Slavery Standard*, an attempt to shame the federal government into recognizing Harriet's service. Abolitionist friends of old sent little sums of money, enough to help Harriet get by, but the federal government remained unmoved. She saw this defeat as temporary, however, and had no intentions of dropping her pursuit for what was rightfully owed to her. Harriet would continue this fight for decades.

TELLING HER STORY

With no promise of a pension, Harriet and her friends began the planning of her memoir, a narrative that would be printed and sold with the hopes of finding a large readership that could generate significant income. A number of narratives written by formerly enslaved men and women had met with great success, so there was hope that Harriet's incredible experiences would encounter the same interest received by the likes of Frederick Douglass and Harriet Jacobs.

Sarah Bradford, a writer of sentimental novels, was persuaded to take on the task of writing Harriet's authorized biography. Unlike Frederick Douglass, Harriet remained illiterate and was unable to write her own narrative, so she relied upon Bradford to write an epic chronicling of her life. She visited with the writer and recounted her experiences from slavery to freedom, but Bradford's efforts fell flat. A planned trip to Europe in the early fall left Bradford only a few short months to complete the book. Uncorrected mistakes and missed opportunities turned an incredible story into a mediocre narrative. Bradford's Northern background and her skepticism about some of Harriet's accounting of slavery weakened the book and reinforced that Bradford was completely ill-equipped to produce the memoir that Harriet deserved.

Although the book was lacking, Bradford

> Harriet Tubman of Auburn, N. Y., celebrated as a colored Union scout and spy, and as having helped to freedom many of her race, was married, at her home, last week, and several old abolitionists were present.

Marriage announcement for Tubman and Nelson Davis.
Massachusetts Spy (*published as*
Massachusetts Weekly Spy), *April 23, 1869.*

included testimonials from well-known friends and public personalities. For Harriet, the most powerful and humbling contribution came from Frederick Douglass. For her friend and fellow fugitive to write with such admiration must have touched her. Douglass wrote:

> *The difference between us is very marked. Most that I have done and suffered in the service of our cause has been in public, and I have received much encouragement at every step of the way. You, on the other hand, have labored in a private way. I have wrought in the day—you in the night. I have had the applause of the crowd and the satisfaction that comes of being approved by the multitude, while the most that you have done has been witnessed by a few trembling, scarred, and foot-sore bondmen and women whom you have led out of the house of bondage, and whose heartfelt "God bless you" has been your only reward. The midnight sky and the silent stars have been the witnesses of your devotion to freedom and of your heroism. Excepting John Brown—of sacred memory—I know of no one who has willingly encountered more perils and hardships to serve our enslaved people than you have.*

Scenes in the Life of Harriet Tubman was published in 1869 and Harriet was supposed to receive $1,200 from book sales—money that she could use to pay down the debt on her mortgage and for other expenses. But it's unclear if Harriet ever received all of the proceeds from her authorized biography. It doesn't appear as though she received a lump-sum payment, which indicates that her white patrons did not trust Harriet's decision-making when it came to financial affairs. She may have received small amounts of money over a stretch of years, but her mortgage on the seven-acre South Street property wasn't paid off until 1873, a full fourteen years after she came into possession of it.

We don't know how Harriet felt about her authorized biography. Perhaps a friend or family member read each page aloud, allowing Harriet to sit with the depiction of her life. She may have disliked Bradford's rendering of her experiences, but more than likely, her humility prevented her from passing judgment on Bradford's work. Harriet was never one to step into the limelight, always preferring to work for the common good in the background. With the publication of her biography, however, there was no hiding from her fame. Her words and life story were now in print for all to read, all but guaranteeing that Harriet's bravery and selflessness would never be forgotten.

A WIFE AND MOTHER

The release of her book wasn't the only newsworthy thing in Harriet's life. A relationship with Nelson Davis blossomed into something more than platonic friendship, and on March 18, 1869, Harriet and Nelson were married at the Auburn Central Presbyterian Church. A reporter described the wedding as a large celebration with many friends and well-known families of Auburn. Now in her late forties, Harriet was legally married for the first time in her life. She paid no mind to the gossip and hateful chatter that doubted Nelson Davis's commitment to his new bride. Harriet was twice his age, and some townspeople believed that Nelson married Harriet so that she could take care of him—a suggestion that the marriage wasn't based upon a reciprocal love. In reality, there were many reasons that men and women married one another in the nineteenth century, and survival was often at the top of the list. Love was a wonderful thing, but for formerly enslaved people who lived fragile lives mired in poverty and the danger of white violence, companionship and mutual support often trumped romantic love. For Harriet and Nelson, there were likely many reasons that the two decided to wed. The couple began to fashion a new life together, one that would last nearly twenty years until the end of his life.

Over the next decade, the farm was at the center of Harriet and Nelson's life. Industrious as ever, they raised chickens, ducks, and pigs, and grew fruits and vegetables. They sold butter and eggs, built a brickyard, and they even contracted with the city of Auburn to collect garbage—slops that were fed to their pigs. Life was never easy, and like many other black families across the nation, Harriet and Nelson lived a life without financial solvency. Sometimes there wasn't enough food for everyone to eat, but Harriet never turned away any men, women, and children in need. With so many people counting on her, she was deeply resentful when she learned that some veterans received up to eight dollars per month from the government. So once again, she leaned upon her Auburn friends to help her apply for a government pension. She might be ignored, but Harriet was not one to abandon a mission.

HARD TIMES

The 1870s were difficult times for black people across the nation. The end of Reconstruction left the nation with little interest in the plight of former slaves, and the birth of groups like the Ku Klux Klan and the Knights of the White Camelia reinforced racial violence from New York to Mississippi. It was a good thing that

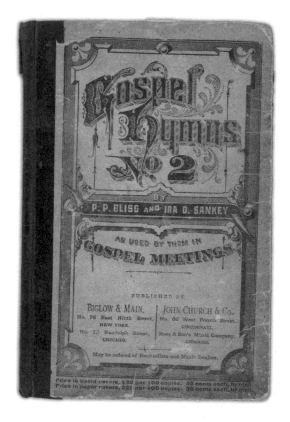

Gospel Hymns No. 2, Personal Hymnal of Harriet Tubman, 1876.

both Harriet and her husband were deeply religious and could find some solace in an active church community. Nelson was heavily involved in St. Mark's AME Church and eventually became a trustee. Harriet may have attended church with him, but later in life she became a devoted member of Auburn's AME Zion Church. They would need spiritual strength to muddle their way through a national depression that lasted for more than two decades. Harriet and Nelson weren't accustomed to having much in the way of material possessions, but the depression nearly squeezed them dry.

Poverty was traumatizing, but the loss of Harriet's father reminded her of what was important in life. Ben Ross (now Stewart) died sometime in 1871. He survived into his mid-eighties, and while his rheumatism and the ravages of old age took their toll, there were also the miracles in his life. The suffering under slavery was heavy, but he lived long enough to witness the end of human bondage. He and his wife Rit managed to stay together for more than half a century, a fact that could only be understood as a blessing. Rit passed away in October of 1880, and as difficult as this may have been, Harriet could take pride in all that she had done for her mother and father. She led them out of Maryland, provided them with food and shelter, and reconnected them with their family. She made certain that they were not alone in their last days. Thanks to Harriet, her parents had lived long lives, and now she needed to shift her attention to other people who needed her most. That now included a daughter named Gertie.

Little is known about the baby girl adopted by Nelson and Harriet in 1874. Gertie's biological background and how she arrived in the care of the Davis family is still a mystery. But as a family they struggled through the ups and downs of life. Harriet's

Postcard of Harriet Tubman, Nelson Davis, and daughter, Gertie, circa 1887.

fame and her reputation of kind-heartedness made her a target within the Auburn community, and on occasion, she was swindled out of money. In 1873, Harriet was scammed out of $2,000 in a gold-for-cash scheme, an incident that left her bruised, bloody, and terribly embarrassed. Convinced by a stranger that he would give her $5,000 in gold for only $2,000 in cash, Harriet borrowed the money from a local real-estate investor so that she could turn a quick profit. She soon figured out that she had been duped when two men robbed and assaulted her. On another occasion, a strange man appeared at Harriet's door asking for assistance, playing upon her reputation as a generous person. Luckily, this time she narrowly escaped another dangerous robbery.

Setbacks, however, never defined her. She knew that God would protect her from devastating harm. So when Harriet's wooden home burned down in the early 1880s, Nelson, a bricklayer, helped to rebuild a stronger and sturdier residence. Life kept throwing punches at the couple, and sometimes the blows landed. But in almost every circumstance, Harriet found a way to get back on her feet and continue providing for her family.

A true test of Harriet's grit and resolve came in October of 1888 when her husband Nelson Davis died at the age of forty-five. After the Civil War, he had lived with shattered health for more than twenty years, and Harriet took care of him from the moment that he appeared on her doorstep in Auburn. She never regretted the attention that she offered to her husband; in fact, it helped her to think about the ways that she could help ill, elderly, and indigent people. She laid her husband to rest in Fort Hill Cemetery.

THE BALLOT BOX

With her parents and husband gone, Harriet turned her attention to reform work. Black women interested in activism often found themselves unable to participate in meaningful ways. Finding steady employment and taking care of family were always prioritized, and in Harriet's case, she spent the last two decades of

Colorized Portrait of Harriet Araminta Tubman,
circa 1885. American Civil War Museum, Richmond, VA.

her life choosing between eating and activism—there really was no choice to be made. Now in her sixties, the widow began to spend time advocating for women's rights. More specifically, she believed that women should have the right to vote, so she connected with her old abolitionist friends who were now focused on suffrage. They welcomed her into the fold.

Harriet wasn't new to this movement. She had thought about and lobbied for women's rights for two decades. In 1860, she gave her first public talk at a suffrage meeting in Boston, and twenty years later, she found herself compelled to once again give her time and energy to the cause. In her later years, Harriet reminisced that she belonged to "Miss Anthony's organization," also known as the National Woman Suffrage Association, founded by Susan B. Anthony. Once the organization merged to become the National American Woman Suffrage Association, Harriet found herself traveling across New York and New England to make appearances on behalf of herself and the organization. She spoke to crowds, large and small, about her experiences as an enslaved woman and compared the imperative to end slavery with the need to give women the right to vote. Harriet told of her time as a union spy and nurse, reminding her audiences that women had been responsible for caring for wounded soldiers and serving the nation. In Harriet's eyes, women were the equal of any man, should be treated with respect and dignity, and given the same rights as male citizens.

She was committed to activism, but Harriet's work with women's rights groups became more difficult as the racial politics of white women suffragists left no place for black women's participation. Many white suffragists were bitter about the Fifteenth Amendment that gave black men the right to vote but left women (both white and black) disenfranchised. Images of black men at the ballot box registered as a sign of their own defeat. Their resentment was palpable, prompting black activists like Frederick Douglass and Frances Ellen Watkins Harper to separate themselves from longtime friends. Generally, Southern white women (and many across the nation) felt at ease with segregation and were more than content with the departure of black activists from white suffragist groups. But for the aging Harriet, it was not so easy to turn her back on the friends who had given her support over the years, even when they publicly denounced black male suffrage. She managed to walk a delicate line—careful not to alienate her white associates as she supported black advancement. Harriet visited with white suffragists up through the twentieth century, but she also joined the ranks of black women activists.

MOTHER TUBMAN

By the 1890s, most black women abandoned the traditional suffragist movement. To them, the calls for sisterhood from white suffragists were drowned out by segregationist banter. Black women weren't going to fight for equal rights alongside white racists, so they formed their own organizations, and

Harriet Tubman; "The Moses of her people"; Herself a fugitive, she abducted more than 300 slaves, and also served as a scout and nurse for the Union Forces, circa 1889.

in 1896 the National Association of Colored Women was founded. Led by their first president, Mary Church Terrell, the NACW became the largest federation of black women's clubs, and although they supported suffrage, they also turned their attention to the problems facing black people in a Jim Crow America. The recent decision handed down by the Supreme Court in the *Plessy v. Ferguson* case made segregation the law of the land, and black women reformers prepared themselves for battles on multiple fronts; suffrage was only one of many demands.

In July of 1896, Harriet was asked to serve as a featured speaker at the first meeting of the NACW. Introduced as "Mother Tubman"—a label of respect for the aging activist—she spoke about her time as a nurse and spy for the army. Harriet told her captive audience about the importance of all reform work, and more specifically, the need to care for the aged and infirm within their community. She hoped that the women in the audience would support her newest project—a home and hospital for elderly and invalid black people. She would need every dollar and every dime to get her project started, so Harriet began actively fundraising for her new mission.

GETTING PAID

While hoping to raise money for her new endeavor—the home for the aged—she also continued to pursue money owed to her by the federal government. In June of 1890, Harriet filed her first claim for a widow's pension provided under the Dependent Pension Act of 1890. She had repeatedly filed and petitioned for her own war pension, but she was denied at every turn. But because Nelson had served as a soldier in the United States Colored Troops, the federal government could not deny Harriet her claim. Still, nothing was easy about this process. Because many

"IT'S ALL ABOUT THE TUBMANS" HARRIET'S FINANCIALS

FIRST REWARD FOR HARRIET'S CAPTURE: $100 in 1849 or $3,326 in today's dollars

HOW MUCH HARRIET'S FATHER PAID TO FREE HER MOTHER: $20

HOW MUCH SHE MADE AS A NURSE DURING THE CIVIL WAR: $0

HARRIET'S MONTHLY PENSION FOR SERVING AS A NURSE IN THE UNION ARMY: $12

THE COST OF HARRIET'S FIRST HOME: $1,200

HARRIET'S WIDOW'S PENSION: $8 per month (She also received a lump-sum payment of $500)

WHAT SOLDIERS RECEIVED FOR THEIR WAR PENSIONS: $8 per month if completely disabled

General Affidavit of Harriet Tubman Davis regarding payment for services rendered during the Civil War, 1898.

formerly enslaved men changed their last names after emancipation, it was often difficult to verify identity. Harriet's husband appeared as "Nelson Charles" on his army records, so his change of name to "Nelson Davis" created a bureaucratic labyrinth. It would take five long years for Harriet to prove Nelson's identity and that their marriage was legally binding. By October of 1895, Harriet was awarded eight dollars a month for her widow's pension and received a $500 payment for five years of back pay. A friend and New York congressman believed that she was owed much more. In 1899, Sereno E. Payne introduced a bill to Congress on her behalf and eventually, Harriet was awarded twenty dollars per month: eight dollars for her widow's pension and twelve dollars for her service as a nurse. She was never compensated for her service as a spy or a scout, but Harriet finally had a secure monthly income. She was seventy-seven years old.

In many ways, Harriet must have felt as though the clock was ticking. She swung into action and began making arrangements for the creation of a home and hospital for the poor and aged. This type of activism—caring for the elderly—was one of the first kinds of organized reform by black women. For more than a century, Northern black women created organizations and raised funds to take care of their aged men and women. Without a social safety net for black people, Harriet stepped in to make certain that the elderly spent their last days with care, comfort, and dignity—just as she had done for her parents. In the spring of 1896,

55TH CONGRESS,
3D SESSION.

H. R. 4982.

[Report No. 1774.]

IN THE HOUSE OF REPRESENTATIVES.

DECEMBER 14, 1897.

Mr. PAYNE introduced the following bill; which was referred to the Committee on Invalid Pensions and ordered to be printed.

JANUARY 19, 1899.

Reported with an amendment, committed to the Committee of the Whole House, and ordered to be printed.

[Amend the title.]

A BILL

Granting a pension to Harriet Tubman Davis, late a nurse in the United States Army.

1   *Be it enacted by the Senate and House of Representa-*
2 *tives of the United States of America in Congress assembled,*
3 That the Secretary of the Interior be, and he is hereby,
4 authorized and directed to place upon the pension roll of the
5 United States the name of Harriet Tubman Davis, late a
6 nurse in the United States Army, and pay her a pension at
7 the rate of twenty-five dollars per month in lieu of all other
8 pensions.

    Amend the title so as to read: "A bill granting an increase of pension to Harriet Tubman Davis."

A bill granting a pension to Harriet Tubman Davis, 1899.

Harriet purchased a twenty-five-acre lot that sat adjacent to her property and began a fundraising campaign in earnest. Even as her health began to decline, she called upon the ministers of her church home, the AME Zion Church, to help her raise additional funds. By 1902, Harriet realized that she would need to let others lead the charge on her dream project. She turned over the deed of the property to the church, hoping they would breathe life into her dream of a home for the aged—and they did just that. In 1908, the Harriet Tubman Home for Aged and Indigent Negroes finally opened its doors.

SERVANT OF GOD

In March of 1913, Woodrow Wilson prepared for his inauguration as the twenty-eighth president of the United States. He arrived in Washington, DC, expecting to meet the typical fanfare and excitement that accompanies the arrival of the president-elect, but the anticipated attention was eclipsed by a strange and unheard-of event. Wilson wasn't greeted by as many adoring citizens as he anticipated. Instead he watched thousands of women descend upon the capital to demand equality and the right to vote.

Women from across the country organized for women's rights, and suffragists like Alice Paul and Lucy Burns led the National American Woman Suffrage Association to plan an unusual parade that would guide thousands of women down Pennsylvania Avenue. The Woman Suffrage Procession of 1913 was the first large political march organized in the nation's capital. The protest centered upon the need for an amendment to the constitution that would offer women the right to vote, a political demand that had been debated nearly sixty-five years earlier at the famed Seneca

Harriet Tubman, circa 1911.

Falls Convention. But in 1913, organizers made the bold decision to march through the capital, reminding politicians and others about the power of women.

For most women, this march was a sign of progress, but for black suffragists, it was a reminder of the disrespect that originally caused them to break ranks from white suffragists. Organizers of the parade decided that black women would be allowed to march; however, they would be relegated to the back of the parade line. Segregation seeped into every aspect of American life—even within progressive protest movements. Some black women agreed to march at the rear of the parade, but respected activist and journalist Ida B. Wells-Barnett refused to submit to racist treatment. She told the delegation from Illinois that she would march with them or not march at all. Wells-Barnett marched with her state delegation, but she was one of only a small number of black women granted this privilege.

Back in Auburn, New York, Harriet Tubman Davis was confined to her bed. She had transitioned to a wheelchair a few years earlier, but by the spring of 1913, pneumonia tightened its grip on the ninety-one-year-old reformer. Cared for by the staff at the Harriet Tubman Home for Aged and Indigent Negroes, Harriet spent her remaining days in the infirmary named after her friend and activist John Brown.

Given her interests in women's suffrage, news of the parade must have reached her. It was covered broadly by the press, with papers reporting on the thousands of women who filled the streets of Washington, DC. If Harriet was lucid, she would've understood the tremendous importance of this march and, of course, felt some measure of pride. She believed deeply in a woman's right to vote, and the last years of her activist life were spent pursuing what she believed to be a right denied. But she wouldn't have been surprised by the blatant display of racism and disrespect at the parade. Even as the nation celebrated the fiftieth anniversary of the Emancipation Proclamation, Harriet and the rest of black

America knew that the shelf life of racism had far from expired. There was still so much work to be done.

Photographic postcard of Harriet Tubman lying in repose in Auburn, New York, March 11, 1913.

One week after the march, before Harriet slipped into a coma, she spoke her final words to a small group of loved ones gathered at her bedside. Her coughing subsided long enough for Harriet to say, "I go away to prepare a place for you, that where I am you also may be." In her final hours, Harriet invoked the book of John from the Bible and thought only about her God and about comforting her friends that she would leave behind. On March 10, 1913, Harriet Tubman Davis joined her ancestors.

• • •

Three days after her death, hundreds of friends and acquaintances traveled to Auburn, New York, to commemorate the life of an American hero. Following a service at the Harriet Tubman Home, her body was taken to Thompson Memorial AME Zion Church, where a thick crowd poured into the building for a final viewing of the woman who had fought against slavery and for women's rights. Mourners shuffled by the casket draped in an American flag, patiently waiting for a last glimpse of the freedom fighter called Moses. Placed in the casket was a commemorative medal given to Harriet by Queen Victoria of England, a gift offered to dignitaries invited to the Queen's Diamond Jubilee. Between her two clasped hands was a crucifix. The church service included dignitaries such as Mary Burnett Talbert, coorganizer of the Niagara Movement (which led to the founding of the NAACP) and future president of the National Association of Colored Women's Clubs. Talbert spoke with deep admiration of Harriet and reminisced about their last encounter—a visit that was both difficult and empowering. Harriet's condition was grave, but even in the final weeks of her life, she found the strength to send a message to women activists across the nation. She told Talbert, *"tell the women to stand together for God will never forsaken* [sic] *us."*

Harriet Tubman Davis was laid to rest at Fort Hill Cemetery with military honors. Her death marked the end of an incredible life, but the citizens of Auburn and activists around the nation were determined to have her spirit and contributions live on. Fundraising efforts began in earnest, and in only a year's time, a bronze tablet was crafted in Harriet's honor. Booker T. Washington, one of the most influential African American intellectuals and philanthropists of his time, traveled to New York to serve as the keynote speaker at the unveiling and eventually, the tablet was placed on the county courthouse in Auburn.

It took many years, but by 1937 black women gathered together at the gravesite of their fallen sister. Determined to give her the respect she was owed, the Empire State Federation of Women's Clubs raised funds to replace the headstone of their war hero and activist. It reads:

To The Memory of Harriet Tubman Davis
Heroine of the Underground Railroad
Nurse and Scout in the Civil War
Born about 1820 in Maryland
Died March 10, 1913 at Auburn, N.Y.
"Servant of God, Well Done"
Erected by the
Empire State Federation of Womens Clubs
July 5, 1937

The memory of Harriet lived on as parents and grandparents shared her courageous story with the next generation of activists. Over dinner tables and in small Sunday school classrooms, black

Harriet Tubman tablet. F. A. Davis Company; Philadelphia, PA, 1916.

folks reached back to the oral tradition of their ancestors, sharing the unbelievable stories and experiences of a woman like no other. Writers, activists, and ministers refused to let Harriet's story be erased by time, and they continued to say her name. Their work paid off. In 1944, the US Maritime Commission recognized Harriet's service to the military by the naming of the *SS Harriet Tubman*, the only Liberty ship to be named for a black woman. A decade later, Harriet's strength and courage emboldened the civil rights workers of the 1950s and 1960s, and teachers across the nation began to include her amazing story in social-studies curricula. Schools, libraries, and museums were named in her honor, dedicating their mission to her life's vision.

Harriet Tubman is now a household name—a symbol of power, strength, and honor.

Harriet Tubman, abolitionist, circa 1900s.

LET ME RAP TO YOU REAL QUICK:

"I was the conductor of the Underground Railroad for eight years, and I can say what most conductors can't say—I never ran my train off the track and I never lost a passenger."

— **HARRIET TUBMAN ADDRESSES A SUFFRAGE CONVENTION, NY, 1896**

"I have seen hundreds of escaped slaves, but I never saw one who was willing to go back and be a slave."

—**HARRIET TUBMAN TO BENJAMIN DREW, ST. CATHARINES, ONTARIO, CANADA, 1855**

"I had reasoned this out in my mind; there was one of two things I had a right to, liberty, or death; if I could not have one, I would have the other; for no man should take me alive; I should fight for my liberty as long as my strength lasted, and when the time came for me to go, the Lord would let them take me."

—**HARRIET TUBMAN TO SARAH BRADFORD IN *HARRIET, THE MOSES OF HER PEOPLE*, 1886**

FAMOUS HARRIET TUBMAN QUOTES

"I have heard their [bondpeople's] groans and sighs, and seen their tears, and I would give every drop of blood in my veins to free them."

—HARRIET TUBMAN TO SARAH BRADFORD IN *SCENES IN THE LIFE OF HARRIET TUBMAN*, 1869

"God's time [Emancipation] is always near. He set the North Star in the heavens; He gave me the strength in my limbs; He meant I should be free."

—HARRIET TUBMAN TO EDNAH DOW CHENEY, NEW YORK CITY, CIRCA 1859

"I think slavery is the next thing to hell. If a person would send another into bondage, he would, it appears to me, be bad enough to send him into hell, if he could."

—HARRIET TUBMAN TO BENJAMIN DREW, ST. CATHARINES, ONTARIO, CANADA, 1855

"If he was weak enough to give out, he'd be weak enough to betray us all, and all who had helped us; and do you think I'd let so many die just for one coward man?"

—HARRIET TUBMAN TO EDNAH DOW CHENEY, SC, 1865

Suggested Readings

Harriet Tubman:

Clinton, Catherine. *Harriet Tubman: The Road to Freedom.* Boston: Little, Brown, 2004.

Conrad, Earl. *Harriet Tubman: Negro Soldier and Abolitionist.* Washington, DC: Associated Publishers, 1943.

Horton, Lois E. *Harriet Tubman and the Fight for Freedom: A Brief History with Documents.* Boston: Bedford/St. Martin's, 2013.

Humez, Jean McMahon. *Harriet Tubman: The Life and the Life Stories.* Madison: University of Wisconsin Press, 2003.

Larson, Kate Clifford. *Bound for the Promised Land: Harriet Tubman, Portrait of an American Hero.* New York: Ballantine Books, 2003.

Lowry, Beverly. *Harriet Tubman: Imagining a Life.* New York: Doubleday, 2007.

Sernett, Milton C. *Harriet Tubman: Myth, Memory, and History.* Durham, NC: Duke University Press, 2007.

Telford, Emma P. "Harriet: The Modern Moses of Heroism and Visions." 1905. *The Telford Manuscript.* Cayuga Museum of History and Art, Auburn, NY.

The Underground Railroad:

Bordewich, Fergus M. *Bound for Canaan: The Epic Story of the Underground Railroad, America's First Civil Rights Movement.* New York: Amistad, 2006.

Foner, Eric. *Gateway to Freedom: The Hidden History of the Underground Railroad.* New York: W.W. Norton & Company, 2015.

Siebert, Wilbur H. *The Underground Railroad from Slavery to Freedom.* New York City: Macmillan, 1898.

Switala, William J. *Underground Railroad in Delaware, Maryland, and West Virginia.* Mechanicsburg, PA: Stackpole Books, 2004.

Fugitive Slaves:

Blackett, R. J. M. *The Captive's Quest for Freedom: Fugitive Slaves, the 1850 Fugitive Slave Law, and the Politics of Slavery.* New York: Cambridge University Press, 2018.

Campbell, Stanley W. *The Slave Catchers: Enforcement of the Fugitive Law, 1850–1860.* Chapel Hill: University of North Carolina Press, 1970.

Dunbar, Erica Armstrong. *Never Caught: The Washingtons' Relentless Pursuit of Their Runaway Slave, Ona Judge.* New York: 37 Ink/Atria, 2017.

Franklin, John Hope, and Loren Schweninger. *Runaway Slaves: Rebels on the Plantation.* New York: Oxford University Press, 1999.

African Americans in Canada:

Broyld, Dann J. "Fannin' Flies and Tellin' Lies: Black Runaways and American Tales of Life in British Canada Before the Civil War." *American Review of Canadian Studies* 44, no. 2 (April 2014): 169–86.

Broyld, Dann J., "'Justice Was Refused Me, I Resolved to Free Myself': John W. Lindsay. Finding Elements of American Freedoms in British Canada, 1805–1876." *Ontario History* 109, no. 1 (Spring 2017): 27–59. https://doi.org/10.7202/1039198a.

Hepburn, Sharon A. Roger. *Crossing the Border: A Free Black Community in Canada.* Chicago: University of Illinois Press, 2007.

Prince, Bryan. *My Brother's Keeper: African Canadians and the American Civil War*. Toronto: Dundurn, 2015.

Rhodes, Jane. *Mary Ann Shadd Cary: The Black Press and Protest in the Nineteenth Century*. Bloomington: Indiana University Press, 1998.

Silverman, Jason H. "The American Fugitive Slave in Canada: Myth and Realities." *Southern Studies, 19,* no. 3 (1980), 215–27.

Silverman, Jason H. *Unwelcome Guests: Canada West's Response to American Fugitive Slaves*. Millwood, NY: Associated Faculty Press, Inc., 1985.

Slavery in Maryland:

Berlin, Ira. *Many Thousands Gone: The First Two Centuries of Slavery in North America*. Cambridge, MA: Belknap Press of Harvard University Press, 1998.

Fields, Barbara Jeanne. *Slavery and Freedom on the Middle Ground: Maryland During the Nineteenth Century*. New Haven, CT: Yale University Press, 1985.

Marks, Carole C. *A History of African Americans of Delaware and Maryland's Eastern Shore*. Wilmington, DE: Delaware Heritage Commission, 1998.

Millward, Jessica. *Finding Charity's Folk: Enslaved and Free Black Women in Maryland*. Athens, GA: University of Georgia Press, 2015.

African Americans and the Civil War:

Berlin, Ira, Joseph P. Reidy, and Leslie S. Rowland. *Freedom's Soldiers: The Black Military Experience in the Civil War*. Cambridge, UK: Cambridge University Press, 1998.

Blatt, Martin Henry, Thomas J. Brown, and Donald Yacovone. *Hope & Glory: Essays on the Legacy of the Fifty-Fourth Massachusetts Regiment*. Amherst: University of Massachusetts in association with Massachusetts Historical Society, Boston, 2001.

Blight, David W. *Race and Reunion: The Civil War in American Memory*. Cambridge, MA: Harvard University Press, 2001.

Eggleston, Larry G. *Women in the Civil War: Extraordinary Stories of Soldiers, Spies, Nurses, Doctors, Crusaders, and Others*. Jefferson, NC: McFarland, 2003.

Massey, Mary Elizabeth. *Women in the Civil War*. Lincoln: University of Nebraska Press, 1994.

Shaffer, Donald. *After the Glory: The Struggles of Black Civil War Veterans*. Lawrence: University Press of Kansas, 2004.

James Montgomery and the Combahee Raid:

Benedict, Bryce D. *Jayhawkers: The Civil War Brigade of James Henry Lane*. Norman: University of Oklahoma Press, 2009.

Dirck, Brian R. "By the Hand of God: James Montgomery and Redemptive Violence," *Kansas History: A Journal of the Central Plains* 27 (Spring–Summer 2004): 100–15.

Grigg, Jeff W. *The Combahee River Raid: Harriet Tubman & Lowcountry Liberation*. Charleston, South Carolina: The History Press, 2014.

John Brown:

Horwitz, Tony. *Midnight Rising: John Brown and the Raid That Sparked the Civil War*. New York: Henry Holt and Co., 2011.

Oates, Stephen B. *To Purge This Land with Blood: A Biography of John Brown*. Amherst: University of Massachusetts, 1984.

Quarles, Benjamin. *Allies for Freedom: Blacks on John Brown*. Cambridge, MA: Da Capo, 2001.

SUGGESTED READINGS

Slavery and Abolition:

Berry, Daina Ramey. *The Price for Their Pound of Flesh: The Value of the Enslaved, from Womb to Grave, in the Building of a Nation.* Boston: Beacon Press, 2017.

Ericson, David F. *The Debate over Slavery: Antislavery and Proslavery Liberalism in Antebellum America.* New York: New York University Press, 2000.

Hahn, Steven. *The Political Worlds of Slavery and Freedom.* Cambridge, MA: Harvard University Press, 2009.

Jackson, Kellie Carter. *Force and Freedom: Black Abolitionists and the Politics of Violence.* Philadelphia: University of Pennsylvania Press, 2019.

Jeffrey, Julie Roy. *The Great Silent Army of Abolitionism: Ordinary Women in the Antislavery Movement.* Chapel Hill: University of North Carolina Press, 1998.

Lowance, Mason I. *Against Slavery: An Abolitionist Reader.* London: Penguin, 2000.

Sernett, Milton C. *North Star Country: Upstate New York and the Crusade for African American Freedom.* Syracuse, NY: Syracuse University Press, 2002.

Sinha, Manisha. *The Slave's Cause: A History of Abolition.* New Haven, CT: Yale University Press, 2016.

Whitman, Stephen T. *Challenging Slavery in the Chesapeake: Black and White Resistance to Human Bondage, 1775–1865.* Baltimore: Maryland Historical Society, 2007.

African American Women and Suffrage:

Free, Laura E. *Suffrage Reconstructed: Gender, Race, and Voting Rights in the Civil War Era.* Ithaca: Cornell University Press, 2015.

Gordon, Anna D., and Bettye Collier-Thomas. *African American Women and the Vote, 1837–1965.* Amherst: University of Massachusetts Press, 1997.

Terborg-Penn, Rosalyn. *African American Women in the Struggle for the Vote, 1850–1920.* Bloomington: Indiana University Press, 1998.

Books for Kids:

Allen, Thomas B., and Carla Bauer. *Harriet Tubman, Secret Agent: How Daring Slaves and Free Blacks Spied for the Union During the Civil War.* Washington, DC: National Geographic, 2006.

Amoroso, Cynthia. *Harriet Tubman: Abolitionist and Underground Railroad Conductor.* Chanhassen, MN: Child's World, 2004.

Cline-Ransome, Lisa. *Before She Was Harriet.* New York: Holiday House, 2017.

Gayle, Sharon. *Harriet Tubman and the Freedom Train.* New York: Aladdin, 2003.

Schraff, Anne E. *Harriet Tubman: Moses of the Underground Railroad.* Berkeley Heights, NJ: Enslow Publishing, 2000.

PHOTO AND ILLUSTRATION CREDITS

* Special Thanks to William Harrison Graves

All illustrations created by Monica Ahanonu. Special thanks to Kate Clifford Larson for the research that produced "Harriet's Moves: Traveling the Underground."

Gospel Hymns No. 2, Personal Hymnal of Harriet Tubman, 1876. Courtesy of the Smithsonian National Museum of African American History and Culture, gift of Charles L. Blockson.

Photographic postcard of Harriet Tubman lying in repose in Auburn, New York, March 11, 1913. Courtesy of the Smithsonian National Museum of African American History and Culture.

Postcard of Harriet Tubman, Nelson Davis, and daughter, Gertie, circa 1887. Courtesy of the Smithsonian National Museum of African American History and Culture, gift of Charles L. Blockson.

William Henry [Ross] Stewart, one of Harriet Tubman's brothers who fled to Canada. Photo probably taken in Canada, circa 1860. Courtesy of Judith G. Bryant and Kate Clifford Larson.

Runaway reward advertisement for Tubman (Minty and her two brothers). *Cambridge Democrat* newspaper, October 3, 1849. Courtesy of Jay and Susan Meredith, Bucktown Village Foundation, Bucktown, Maryland.

Marriage announcement for Tubman and Nelson Davis. *Massachusetts Spy* (published as *Massachusetts Weekly Spy*), April 23, 1869. Courtesy of American Antiquarian Society, Worcester, MA.

Harriet Tubman; "The Moses of her people"; Herself a fugitive, she abducted more than 300 slaves, and also served as a scout and nurse for the Union forces, circa 1889. Courtesy of the Schomburg Center for Research in Black Culture, Jean Blackwell Hutson Research and Reference Division.

Harriet Tubman, abolitionist, circa 1900s. Courtesy of the Schomburg Center for Research in Black Culture, Photographs and Prints Division.

Harriet Tubman tablet. F. A. Davis Company, Philadelphia, PA, 1916. Courtesy of the Schomburg Center for Research in Black Culture, Jean Blackwell Hutson Research and Reference Division.

General Affidavit of Harriet Tubman Davis regarding payment for services rendered during the Civil War, 1898. Records of the US House of Representatives. Courtesy of the National Archives.

A bill granting a pension to Harriet Tubman Davis, 1899. Records of the US House of Representatives, Courtesy of the National Archives.

Colorized Portrait of Harriet Araminta Tubman, circa 1885. Courtesy of the American Civil War Museum, Richmond, VA. National Portrait Gallery, Smithsonian Institution.

Portrait of Harriet Tubman, Auburn, New York, circa 1868. Courtesy of the Library of Congress and the National Museum of African American History and Culture.

Harriet Tubman, circa 1911. Courtesy of the Library of Congress.

Harriet Tubman, between circa 1871–1876. Courtesy of the Library of Congress.

Photos of Dorchester County, Eastern Shore, MD. Courtesy of Mindie Burgoyne.

Sojourner Truth, 1864. Courtesy of the Library of Congress.

Shaw's nurse at memorial (*Boston Herald*, May 31, 1905). Courtesy of the Boston Athenæum. A special thanks to Kate Clifford Larson and Ryan McNabb.

The redesign of the twenty-dollar bill featuring Harriet Tubman that was slotted for a 2020 unveiling has been delayed. As of this writing, there are no plans to unveil the new bill before 2028. @TubmanStamp

NOTES

Author's Note

xi. *lay motionless as a log, mumbling prayers through teeth clenched on the bullet*: Samuel Adams Hopkins, *Grandfather Stories* (New York: Random House, 1947), 277.

Introduction

xiv. "if he was weak enough to give out, he'd be weak enough to betray us all, and all who had helped us; and do you think I'd let so many die just for one coward man?" Ednah Dow Littlehale Cheney, "Moses," *Freedmen's Record*, March 1865, 36.

xiv. *He could keep moving or he could die*: Sarah Hopkins Bradford, *Harriet: The Moses of Her People* (New York: G.R. Lockwood, 1886), 33. Sarah H. Bradford, *Scenes in the Life of Harriet Tubman* (Auburn, NY: W. J. Moses, 1869), 25. Tubman gave multiple reports about similar situations, some involving a group of fugitives, some involving a single individual. In Sarah Bradford's text, we must remember that this account was given by Tubman to Bradford. We don't know if Tubman used this language or if Bradford offered embellishment—complete with racial epithets. I chose to paraphrase.

PART I: MINTY'S STORY

The Alpha Journey

6. *Her enslaver was a man named Atthow Pattison and once he concluded the purchase, he took her to his farm. He would name her Modesty*: Catherine Clinton, *Harriet Tubman: The Road to Freedom* (Boston: Little, Brown, 2004), 5; Paul Touart, "Monograph on Harriet Tubman," Maryland Historical Trust Library, 3.

7. *Modesty probably made a direct voyage from Africa on a British-owned ship*: Lorena S. Walsh, "The Chesapeake Slave Trade: Regional Patterns, African Origins, and Some Implications," *The William and Mary Quarterly* 58, no. 1 (January 2001): 148. For information on African Americans in mainland British America living in the Chesapeake region, see: Phillip Morgan, *Slave Counterpoint: Black Culture in the Eighteenth-Century Chesapeake and Lowcountry* (Chapel Hill: University of North Carolina Press, 1998).

7. *Many were kidnapped from towns and villages in present-day Sierra Leone, Liberia, and Ghana*: Lorena S. Walsh, "The Differential Cultural Impact of Free and Coerced Migration to Colonial America," in *Coerced and Free Migration: Global Perspectives*, ed. David Eltis (Stanford, CA: Stanford University Press, 2002), 131.

First Generation American

7–8. *and protected his 265-acre farm that sat on the east side of the Little Blackwater River*: See Kate Clifford Larson, *Bound for the Promised Land: Harriet Tubman, Portrait of an American Hero* (New York: Ballantine Books, 2003), 7–9.

9. "I give and bequeath to my granddaughter Mary Pattison, One Negro girl named Rittia and her increase until she and they arrive to forty-five as would any of her issue born while she was a slave": Atthow Pattison, will dated January 18, 1791, Records of the Dorchester County Chancery, Case 249, October 7, 1853, Maryland State Archives (MDSA).

9. *After inheriting Rit . . . she married Joseph Brodess, a farmer with his own land . . . on March 19, 1800*: Clinton, *Harriet Tubman*, 6; Calvin W. Mowbray and Maurice D. Rimpo, *Close-ups of Early Dorchester County History* (Silver Spring, MD: Family Line Publications, 1987), 40–49.

Dear Mama

12. *she wed the widower Anthony Thompson. He would bring his three young sons and nine slaves to the union*: Larson, *Bound for the Promised Land*, 9.

We Are Family

14. *Some six years later, on March 15, 1822 a midwife was called to Rit's bedside*: Larson, *Bound for the Promised Land*, 16; Also see: Sarah H. Bradford, *Scenes in the Life of Harriet Tubman* (Auburn, NY: W. J. Moses, 1869). There is much contention among historians surrounding the accounting of Harriet Tubman's birth. Yet, drawing on court records, newspaper advertisements, and early biographies on Tubman, Kate Larson's research and analysis is compelling.

15. *Minty was a toddler when her big sister was sold and taken away*: Edward Brodess to Dempsey P. Kane, July 1825, Dorchester County Land Records, vol. Liber 9 ER 624 p. 625, MDSA. Also see: Larson, *Bound for the Promised Land*, 20. The records list Mariah Ritty as "Rhody" instead of "Ritty," which is likely a mistake or perhaps a nickname used by her owner.

Flesh for Rent

16. "When I was four or five years old, my mother cooked up to the big house and left me to take care of the baby my little brother": Emma Telford, "Harriet: The Modern Moses of Heroism and Visions," as quoted in Larson, *Bound for the Promised Land*, 20.

17. *Hired out to James Cook and his wife*: Bradford, *Scenes*, 73. Tubman was hired out to local planter, James Cook. According to census records, Cook owned seven slaves: two young boys; one young man and elderly man; and four female slaves, including one under ten and three older women. Cook's own family was comprised of a young white woman and two toddler boys.

17. "When we got there, they was at table eating supper. I never eat in the house where white people was and I was ashamed to stand up and eat before them": Telford, "Harriet: The Modern Moses of Heroism and Visions," 4.

18. *Many farmers on the Eastern Shore of Maryland*. Franklin Sanborn, "Harriet Tubman," *The Commonwealth*, Boston, July 17, 1863; Bradford, *Scenes*, 73. Muskrats were a valuable commodity, sought after for both their meat and pelts. See also Frank R. Smith, *Muskrat Investigations in Dorchester County, MD, 1930–1934* (Washington, DC: United States Department of Agriculture, 1938).

20. *She removed the whip from her mantel*. Bradford, *Scenes*, 11–13. It is unclear if Miss Susan lived in the Cook household and there is no evidence to suggest that Mrs. Cook carried the first name of "Susan." The violent exchange between Tubman and unidentified Miss Susan probably indicates that she was hired out to more than one home.

20. "An that baby was always in my lap except when it was asleep, or its mother was feedin it.": Sarah H. Bradford, *Harriet: The Moses of Her People*. (New York: J.J. Little & Co., 1901), 135. An additional chapter was added to the reprinting of the book titled, *"Some Additional Incidents in the Life of 'Harriet.'"*

21. "I was so starved I knowed I'd got to go back to my Missus, I hadn't got no where else to go, but I know'd what was coming": Ibid. 136.

Head Trauma

23. "It cut a piece of that shawl clean off and drove it into my head. They carried me to the house all bleeding and fainting. I had no bed, no place to lie down on at all, and they lay me on the seat of a loom, and I stayed there all that day and the next.": Telford, "Harriet," 6.

24. "I went to work again and there I worked with the blood and sweat rolling down my face till I couldn't see": Ibid.

Innervisions

25. "The rudest of labors,—[I] drove oxen, carted, and plowed and did all the work of a man.": Bradford, *Scenes*, 75.

26. *Ben Ross became a free man in 1841*: Anthony Thompson, Last Will and Testament, Register of Wills, Dorchester County Courthouse, estate no. 0-65-C, Cambridge, MD. During the period, it was common practice to unlawfully extend bondpeople's terms of service beyond the age

of forty-five, the legal age limit for manumission in Maryland. Born in the 1780s, Ross would have been in his fifties at the time of his manumission. More unusual is the material support—including land and a source of trade—willed to Ross for his additional years of labor. Also see: Thomas Bacon, *Laws of Maryland at large, with proper indexes: Now first collected into one compleat body, and published from the original acts and records, remaining in the Secretary's-office of the said province: Together with notes and other matters, relative to the constitution thereof, extracted from the provincial records : To which is prefixed, the charter, with an English translation* (Annapolis, MD: Jonas Green, 1765), 686; Jeffrey R. Brackett, *The Negro in Maryland: A Study of the Institution of Slavery* (1889; reprint, New York: Negro Universities Press, 1969), Barbara Jeanne Fields, *Slavery and Freedom on the Middle Ground: Maryland During the Nineteenth Century* (New Haven: Yale University Press, 1985); Larson, *Bound for the Promised Land*, 68; Sumner Eliot Matison, "Manumission by Purchase," *The Journal of Negro History* 33, no. 2 (1948): 146–67. https://doi .org/10.2307/2715069.

The Ultimate Loss

26. "Oh my children! My poor children!": Interview with James Seward, in Benjamin Drew, *A North-Side View of Slavery. The Refugee: or the Narratives of Fugitive Slaves in Canada. Related by Themselves, with an Account of the History and Condition of the Colored Population of Upper Canada* (Boston: John P. Jewett and Company, 1856), 41.

Love and Marriage

32. "I changed my prayer, and I said 'Lord, if you ain't never going to change that man's heart, kill him . . .'": Bradford, *Scenes*, 14-15.

The Auction Block

32. "Next thing I heard old master was dead, and he died just as he lived. Oh, then, it appeared like I'd give all the world full of gold, if I had it to bring that poor soul back. But I couldn't pray for him no longer": Bradford, *Scenes*, 15.

33. *sold to a local merchant for three hundred and seventy-five dollars*: Thomas Willis, from John Mills and Eliza Brodess, Dorchester County Circuit Court, Chattel Records, 1852–1860, vol. 776, MDSA, 259.

34. *Brodess's widow had placed an advertisement*: Eliza Ann Brodess, "Three Hundred Dollars Reward," *Cambridge Democrat* (Cambridge, MD), October 3, 1849.

34. *Ben and Henry dragged their sister back to the farm.*: Bradford, *Scenes*, 16.

35. "I had reasoned this out of my mind; there was one of two things I had the right to, liberty or death; if I could not have one, I would have the other": Bradford, *Harriet*, 29.

She's Out

36. *Quakers openly opposed slavery*: On Quakerism, Abolition, and Maryland, see: Kenneth L. Carroll, "Maryland Quakers and Slavery," *Quaker History* 72, no. 1 (1983): 27–42. http://www.jstor.org.proxy.libraries.rutgers .edu/stable/41946978; Kenneth L. Carroll, *Quakerism on the Eastern Shore.* (Baltimore: Maryland Historical Society, 1970). Also see: Brycchan Carey and Geoffrey Gilbert Plank, eds., *Quakers and Abolition* (Urbana: University of Illinois Press, 2014). Eighteenth-century Quakers, members of the Religious Society of Friends, were among the earliest organized abolitionists, asserting that enslavement was a violation of Christian principles.

38. *Many fugitives never owned a pair of shoes*: See: David W. Blight, *Passages to Freedom: The Underground Railroad in History and Memory* (Washington, DC: Smithsonian Books, 2004); Fergus M. Bordewich, *Bound for Canaan: The Epic Story of the Underground Railroad, America's First Civil Rights Movement* (New York: Amistad, 2006); Eric Foner, *Gateway to Freedom: The Hidden History of the Underground Railroad* (New York: W. W. Norton & Company, 2015); Benjamin Quarles, *Black Abolitionists* (New York: Oxford University Press, 1969); John Hope Franklin and Loren Schweninger, *Runaway Slaves: Rebels on the Plantation* (New York: Oxford University Press, 1999); William J. Switala, *Underground Railroad in Delaware, Maryland,*

and *West Virginia* (Mechanicsburg, PA: Stackpole Books, 2004). For first-person accounts of the Underground Railroad, see: Charles Blockson, *Underground Railroad, First Person Narratives of Escapes to Freedom in the North* (New York: Prentice Hall, 1987); Drew, *The Refugee*; Eber M. Pettit, *Sketches in the History of the Underground Railroad* (Fredonia, NY: W. McKinstry & Son, 1879); Thomas Smallwood, *A Narrative of Thomas Smallwood (Colored Man): Giving an Account of His Birth—The Period He Was Held in Slavery—His Release—and Removal to Canada, etc. Together with an Account of the Underground Railroad* (Toronto: Smallwood; James Stephens, 1851); William Still, *The Underground Railroad: A Record of Facts, Authentic Narratives, Letters, etc.* (1871 reprint, Chicago: Johnson Publishing Company, Inc., 1970). Samuel Ringgold Ward, *Autobiography of a Fugitive Negro: His Anti-Slavery Labors in the United States, Canada, and England* (London: John Snow, 1855). On the Fugitive Slave Act, see: Stanley W. Campbell, *The Slave Catchers: Enforcement of the Fugitive Law, 1850–1860* (Chapel Hill: University of North Carolina Press, 1970). The Underground Railroad was formed in the early nineteenth century, reaching its height between 1850 and 1860—the period in which Tubman conducted her own missions. Given the clandestine nature of the system, much of what is known about the Underground Railroad is difficult to verify. While there is some debate among scholars, it is believed that between 25,000 to 100,000 enslaved people escaped using the network. The majority of the slaves came from states in the upper south that bordered free states such as Maryland, Kentucky, and Virginia. Though many would try, very few managed to escape from the Deep South.

38. *For most, they'd be physically bound to their children*: Erica Armstrong Dunbar, *Never Caught: The Washingtons' Relentless Pursuit of Their Runaway Slave, Ona Judge* (New York : 37 Ink/Atria Books, 2017), 102; David W. Blight, "Why the Underground Railroad, and Why Now? A Long View," in David W. Blight, ed., *Passages to Freedom: The Underground Railroad in History and Memory* (Washington, DC: Smithsonian Books, 2004), 243; Top of Form; Henry Louis Gates, *100 Amazing Facts About the Negro* (New York:

Pantheon, 2014), 73–76. Eighty percent of fugitives were young males in their teens and twenties who typically fled alone. Between 1838 and 1860, 95 percent absconded alone. Most fugitives were between the ages of sixteen and thirty-five, the period that enslaved women tended to be pregnant, nursing, or caring for children. Young women were far less likely to run away due to attachment to family, reproductive demands imparted by owners, and the difficulty of traveling long distances undetected with infants and toddlers. Whole families with children did attempt flights to freedom, but such efforts were rare.

39. "There was no one to welcome me to the land of freedom. I was a stranger in a strange land; and my home, after all, was down in Maryland; because my father, my mother, my brothers, and sisters, and friends were there. But I was free and they should be free": Bradford, *Scenes*, 20.

PART II: SHE AIN'T SORRY

The Conductor

44. *pick up work in private homes and hotels. During the summer months, she traveled to the resort town of Cape May, New Jersey, to make extra money from vacationers*: Bradford, *Scenes*, 20.

45. *Harriet learned that her niece Kessiah was slotted for the auction block at the Cambridge courthouse*: Larson, *Bound for the Promised Land*, 89; "Harriet Tubman Underground Railroad Routes," Wilbur H. Siebert Underground Railroad Collection, Ohio History Center Archives and Library, https://www.ohiomemory.org/digital/collection/siebert/id/26822/rec/3.

46. *Enslaved women were often examined without their clothing giving male buyers an opportunity to assess and judge their genitalia*: See Deirdre Cooper Owens, *Medical Bondage: Race, Gender, and the Origins of American Gynecology* (Athens, GA: The University of Georgia Press, 2017).

47. *John Bowley, Kessiah's free black husband, . . . managed to smuggle his wife and children out of Dorchester County via*

boat, ferrying them the ninety miles to the bustling seaport of Baltimore: Larson, *Bound for the Promised Land*, 89–90. Some of the details regarding Kessiah's escape are based primarily upon family tradition and folklore and not necessarily confirmed through documentary evidence.

47–48. *Harriet rescued her brother, probably Moses, and two other young men*: Telford, "Harriet: The Modern Moses of Heroism and Visions."

Betrayal

50. *Tubman hit reset on his life and married another woman, a free Black woman named Caroline*: Catherine A. Latimer, "Harriet Tubman," *The Negro History Bulletin* 5, no. 2 (November 1941): 40, JSTOR; Larson, http://www .harriettubmanbiography.com; Ednah Dow Littlehale Cheney, "Moses," *Freedmen's Record*, March 1865, 35.

50. "go right in and make all the trouble she could": Cheney, "Moses," 35.

50. "If he could do without her, she could do without him": Ibid.

Expats

51. "I wouldn't trust Uncle Sam with my people no longer, but I brought 'em [clar] off to Canada": Bradford, *Scenes*, 27.

51. *Harriet and her party of eleven would now be fugitives* and *expats*: "Dred Scott v. Sandford," 60 US 393 (1857). Oyez. Accessed July 7, 2019. https://www.oyez.org/cases/1850 -1900/60us393; Sharon Cromwell, *Dred Scott v. Sandford: A Slave's Case for Freedom and Citizenship* (Minneapolis, MN: Compass Point Books, 2009). The Dred Scott decision was a legal case in which the US Supreme Court on March 6, 1857, ruled that an enslaved man (Dred Scott) who had lived in a free state and territory—where slavery was barred—was not entitled to his freedom, on the basis that a "negro, whose ancestors were imported into [the US], and sold as slaves," whether free or enslaved, could not be an American citizen and therefore failed to have standing to litigate in federal court. The court also decided that

the Missouri Compromise was unconstitutional and that slaves were property under the Fifth Amendment, asserting that any law that would deny a slave owner of that property was unconstitutional.

51. *"On one occasion I had eleven fugitives at the same time under my roof, and it was necessary for them to remain with me until I could collect sufficient money to get them on to Canada"*: Frederick Douglass, *Life and Times of Frederick Douglass, Written by Himself. His Early Life as a Slave, His Escape from Bondage, and His Complete History to the Present Time* (Hartford, CT: Park Publishing, 1882), 329.

51. *traveled to Albany or Rochester, New York, one of the last stations on the Underground before crossing into Canada*: "Harriet Tubman Underground Railroad Routes," William H. Siebert Underground Railroad Collection, Ohio History Center Archives and Library, https://www .ohiomemory.org/digital/collection/siebert/id/26822/rec/2.

54. *bounty hunters would sneak across the border with a goal of retrieving fugitives*: "Correspondence for the Provincial Freeman St. Catharines," *Provincial Freeman*, September 15, 1855; "A Word of Friendly Counsel," *Voice of the Fugitive*, April 9, 1851; H. U. Johnson, *From Dixie to Canada; Romance and Realities of the Underground Railroad* (Buffalo, NY: Charles Well Moulton, 1894); Robin William Winks, *The Blacks in Canada: A History* (Montreal: McGill-Queen's University Press, 2003).

56. *signaled to potential customers, artfully displaying their wares in individual stalls*: Rosemary Sadlier, *Harriet Tubman: Freedom Seeker, Freedom Leader* (Toronto: Dundurn Press, 2012), 86; "Coloured Town—Geneva St. & North St.," *The Underground Railroad: St. Catharines*, http://www.freedomtrail.ca/st_catharines/colortown.htm; William Wells Brown, "The Colored People of Canada," *The Pine and Palm* (Boston), November 30, 1861, in C. Peter Ripley, et al., eds. *The Black Abolitionist Papers.* (Chapel Hill: University of North Carolina Press, 1985), 464.

56. *haggled with patrons over chickens, bacon, butter and a wide variety of fruits and vegetables*: William Wells Brown,

"The Colored People of Canada," 464. Thank you to Ashley Council for her helpful research and writing about fugitive life in Canada.

57. "I have seen hundreds of escaped slaves, but I never saw one who was willing to go back and be a slave": Drew, *The Refugee*, 30.

58. *By 1854, Harriet had made at least five trips back to the Eastern Shore and had rescued close to thirty enslaved people*: Clinton, *Harriet Tubman*, 86.

Who You Gonna Call?

58. *she decided to sell the three siblings on the Monday following Christmas*: Larson, *Bound for the Promised Land*, 110–113; Bradford, *Scenes*, 58.

58. "the good old ship of Zion comes along": Bradford, *Scenes*, 57.

59. *"he accompanied them some miles upon their journey. They then bade him farewell, and left him standing blind-fold in the middle of the road. When he could no longer hear their footsteps, he took off the handkerchief, and turned back"*: Bradford, *Scenes*, 61.

60. *sent to a home in Chester County, Pennsylvania, and from there they were shuttled to William Still's Anti-Slavery office in Philadelphia*: Thomas Miller to J. Miller McKim, December 29, 1854, in Still, *The Underground Railroad*, 305.

60. *Of the thirteen trips she made to Maryland*: Historically, accounts of the number of missions Tubman conducted as well as the number of lives she saved from bondage have varied greatly—often to the point of exaggeration. Some estimates suggest as many as nineteen trips and three hundred people, while Tubman's own count appears to be around eight to nine rescues and fifty to sixty people. Documentary evidence, spanning from Maryland to Canada, identifies approximately thirteen trips and sixty to seventy individuals directly assisted. As Larson points out, we can name nearly every person that Tubman aided to freedom. However, given the secretive nature of work on the Underground Railroad and the resulting limited evidence, we will likely never have a definitive count.

She Came to Slay

61. *Harriet placed the babies in a basket*: Bradford, *Harriet* (1901), 33.

Fearless

62. *Her fluttering heart always notified her when something or someone was a threat; she believed it was a built in message from God*: Bradford, *Scenes*, 50.

62. *literally gave the clothes off her back*: Ibid.

63. *Harriet used blunt force to knock out her own front teeth*: Bradford, *Scenes*, 51; Larson, *Bound for the Promised Land*, 129; Joseph D. Thomas and Marsha McCabe, eds., *Spinner: People and Culture in Southeastern Massachusetts* (New Bedford, MA: Spinner Publications, Inc., 1988), 4:72. There are discrepancies about the extraction of her front teeth, but we know from a number of descriptions of Tubman that she was indeed missing some of her top front teeth.

65. *sell his wife to him for twenty dollars*: "Benjamin Ross Paid Eliza Brodess," *Dorchester County Court Chattel Records, 1847–1852*, Vol. 805, 163.

65. *no person of African descent was entitled to the status of citizen*: Martha S. Jones, *Birthright Citizens: A History of Race and Rights in Antebellum America* (New York: Cambridge University Press, 2018), 128–145.

66. *traveled farther north to Rochester, New York, where they stayed with one of Frederick Douglass's close associates for a few weeks before finally arriving in St. Catharines*: Caroline Bloss Webb letter to Wilbur Siebert, September 7, 1896, in Wilbur H. Siebert Underground Railroad Collection, Ohio History Center Archives and Library, https://www.ohiomemory.org/digital/collection/siebert/id/16211; Larson, *Bound for the Promised Land*, 144.

66. *shed their former surname*: Larson, *Bound for the Promised Land*, 115–116. Stewart was the name of one of Dorchester County's most prominent slaveholding families. It is unclear their motives in choosing this name. However, Larson speculates that it may have been a claim to an undocumented familial relation with the Stewarts of Dorchester or an effort to project power and wealth in spirit as they embraced freedom, like their white counterparts.

Antislavery Agitator

68. *If these new colleagues recognized their faces*: Bradford, *Scenes*, 81.

Homeowner

69. *Harriet knew the antislavery governor*: Seward agreed to provide a home for Tubman's niece, Margaret, one of the many family members she shuttled out of Maryland during the Civil War. There is some controversy over the nature of Margaret's arrival in New York. Margaret's daughter Alice Lucas Brickler would later state that Margaret was kidnapped by Harriet Tubman and that she was actually born of free parents. While we cannot discount the testimony of Alice, the kidnapping of a child during the Civil War runs counterintuitive to everything we know about Tubman. For Brickler's account, see: Alice Lucas Brickler to Earl Conrad, July 19, 1939, Earl Conrad/ Harriet Tubman Collection, New York Public Library, Schomburg Center for Research in Black Culture.

69–70. *With a twenty-five dollar down payment and a promise to make ten-dollar quarterly payments*: Rebecca Green, "History of Harriet Tubman and Her Brick House," Cornell University, Ithaca, New York, 1998.

The General

70. *he would call her "General."*: F. B. Sanborn, ed., *Life and Letters of John Brown, Liberator of Kansas and Martyr of Virginia* (Boston: Roberts Brothers, 1885), 452–453.

72. *Brown paid Harriet twenty-five dollars in gold to support her recruitment efforts throughout the spring and summer.*: Earl Conrad, *Harriet Tubman* (Washington, DC: The Associated Publishers, 1943), 116.

74. *During a Fourth of July presentation, Harriet kept her audience spellbound and collected close to forty dollars . . . for her new comrade*: William Wells Brown, *The Rising Son; or, The Antecedents and Advancement of the Colored Race* (Boston: A. G. Brown & Company, 1874), 536; Clinton, *Harriet Tubman*, 131; *The Liberator*, Boston, July 8, 1858.

One Last Time

75. *there was still a bounty on her head ranging upwards of 12,000.*: The actual amount of the bounty on Harriet Tubman's head is still debated. The $12,000 quote is most likely inflated.

76. *"colored woman of the name Moses"*: "Woman's Rights Meeting," *The Liberator*, Boston, July 6, 1860.

76. *She asked him to make good on an earlier promise*: Harriet Tubman to Wendell Phillips, August 4, 1860, Wendell Phillips Paper, MS Am 1953, (1236). Houghton Library, Harvard College Library.

77. *she had to leave the children behind.* Cheney, "Moses," 35.

77. *The runaways would celebrate New Year's Day of 1861*: Still, *The Underground Railroad*, 554. Also see: Larson, *Bound for the Promised Land*, 185. Still's report of Stephen's last name as "Ennets" is most likely an error or manipulation. This entry is likely referencing the Ennals family, a common surname in Dorchester County. There are no Ennets in Dorchester County.

78. *a new country that would continue the tradition*: See: William C. Davis, *A Government of Our Own: The Making of the Confederacy* (New York: Free Press, 1994); Colin Edward Woodward, *Marching Masters: Slavery, Race, and the Confederate Army During the Civil War* (Charlottesville: University of Virginia Press, 2014).

78. *The Fugitive Aid Society was run by Harriet's trusted family and friends*: See "Relief of Fugitives in Canada," *The Liberator*, Boston, October 25, 1861; "Relief of Fugitives in Canada. An Association," *The Liberator*, Boston, December 20, 1861.

My People Are Free

79. *though black men were not initially allowed to enlist*: Eric Foner, *The Fiery Trial: Abraham Lincoln and American Slavery* (New York: W. W. Norton, 2012); John David Smith, *Lincoln and the U.S. Colored Troops* (Carbondale, IL: Southern Illinois University Press, 2013).

79. "You'll see it, and you'll see it soon. My people are free! My people are free:" Bradford, *Harriet*, 93.

PART III: BAWSS LADY

War Zone

84. *only when a dire need for additional manpower*: Often overshadowed by Lincoln's slowly arrived-at emancipation policy, the confiscation acts—wartime measures initiated by the US Senate—were critical to the effort to abolish slavery and, arguably, represented a precursor to Lincoln's resolution to emancipate slaves by military decree in 1863. The Confiscation Act of 1861 authorized the seizure of all property that was utilized in aid of the rebellion, including the enslaved. Debates over the constitutionality of the first act and whether it went far enough, as well as uneven enforcement prompted the passage of the second Confiscation Act of 1862. This act far exceeded the previous, identifying Confederate slaves "captives of war" who were to be "forever free." Further, Congress extended this policy to include any enslaved person owned by any disloyal master, not just those employed by the Confederate military. Abraham Lincoln opposed the Acts, fearing that they could potentially push border states—particularly Missouri and Kentucky—into secession. Beyond the ideological contests over the saliency of emancipation, these acts were largely aimed at crippling the Confederacy via federal sanctions and expanding Union forces. "The Second Confiscation Act: CHAP. CXCV.–An Act to suppress Insurrection, to punish Treason and Rebellion, to seize and confiscate the Property of Rebels, and for other Purposes," http://www.freedmen .umd.edu/conact2.htm; "Landmark Legislation: The Confiscation Acts of 1861 and 1862," https://www.senate .gov/artandhistory/history/common /generic/ConfiscationActs.htm. Also see: Silvana R. Siddali, *From Property to Person: Slavery and the Confiscation Acts, 1861–1862* (Baton Rouge: Louisiana State University Press, 2005); John James Syrett, *The Civil War Confiscation Acts: Failing to Reconstruct the South* (New York: Fordham University Press, 2005).

84. *For more than a decade, she had been in the business of emancipating people, and the new president appeared hesitant to follow suit*: Interview with Helen W. Tatlock (Mrs. William Tatlock), Earl Conrad/Harriet Tubman Collection, New York Public Library, Schomburg Center for Research in Black Culture. Tadlock asserts that: "During the war she [Harriet] had been opposed to some of the things Lincoln did; she had been prejudiced against him at first." Also see Rosa Belle Holt, "A Heroine in Ebony," *The Chautauquan*, July 1896, 462: "I didn't like Lincoln in those days. I used go see Missus Lincoln but I never wanted to see him. You see we colored people didn't understand then he was our friend. All we knew was that the first colored troops sent south from Massachusetts only got seven dollars a month, while the white regiment got fifteen. We didn't like that." Also see: Larson, *Bound for the Promised Land*, 196. On more than one occasion, Tubman expressed displeasure over Lincoln's stance on "contrabands" and his failure to abolish slavery.

84. *Harriet was introduced to John Andrew*: Charles P. Wood, "Manuscript History Concerning the Pension Claim of Harriet Tubman," HR 55A-D1, Papers Accompanying the Claim of Harriet Tubman, Record Group 233, National Archives, Washington, DC. Also see: Brian McGinty, *John Brown's Trial* (Cambridge, MA: Harvard University Press, 2009), 121.

85. *"she would be a valuable person to operate within the enemies* [sic] *lines in procuring information and scouts:"* Wood, "Manuscript History Concerning the Pension Claim of Harriet Tubman."

85. *also an opportunity to help former slaves begin anew*: "Harriet Tubman," *The Liberator*, Boston, February 21, 1862. Tubman went to various locations around Boston to raise money for the trip to Port Royal.

86. "I first took charge of the Christian Commission house at Beaufort": Telford, "Harriet," 16. Also see: James M. McPherson, *Battle Cry of Freedom: The Civil War Era* (New York: Ballantine Books, 1988), 483.

87. *With meager rations, Union soldiers always complained about hunger so they looked to freedwomen to turn their foraged wild pigs and sheep into freshly cooked dinners*: Kristen Tegtmeier Oertel, *Harriet Tubman: Slavery, the Civil War, and Civil Rights in the Nineteenth Century* (New York: Routledge, 2015), 60–61.

87. *started selling pies and root beer to hungry soldiers*: Bradford, *Scenes*, 37–38.

90. *baking upward of fifty pies an evening, large quantities of gingerbread, and two casks of root beer*: Ibid.

90. *Harriet made her way to Savan House*: See: "Testimony of Harriet Tubman in Court Martial of Pvt. John E. Webster, June 5, 1863," National Archives, quoted in full in Benjamin Guterman, "Doing 'Good Brave Work': Harriet Tubman's Testimony at Beaufort, South Carolina." "Prologue," *Quarterly of the National Archives and Records Administration* 32, no. 3 (2000): 163. It appears that Tubman stayed at the Savan House for part of her time in Beaufort.

Black Moses

91. *Harriet slipped in and out of enemy territory, listening and watching closely, eventually returning to repeat many things the Union officers were glad to know.*: "The Moses of Her People: Proposed Memorial to Harriet Tubman, A Negress," *The Sun*, New York, May 2, 1909; "Harriet Tubman," *The Commonwealth*, July 10, 1863; Bradford, *Scenes*, 38–42.

91. *Their plan was to cut off the stream of supplies that fed and clothed Southern Soldiers and to liberate as many enslaved people as their ship could carry*: William L. Apthorp, "Montgomery's Raids in Florida, Georgia, and South Carolina," Apthorp Family Papers, 1741–1964. Historical Museum of Southern Florida; General Affidavit of Harriet Tubman Davis regarding payment for services rendered during the Civil War, c. 1898, page 1 RG 233, Records of the US House of Representatives; Bradford, *Scenes*, 38–42.

92. *destroying everything in sight*: Apthorp, "Montgomery's Raids in Florida, Georgia, and South Carolina;" Report of Capt. John F. Lay, G. 8. Army, Inspector of Cavalry, Hdqtrs. Dept. South Carolina, Georgia, and Florida, Charleston, 8. C. 7 June 24, 1863. *Official History of the War of the Rebellion*, series 1, vol. xiv, 301, William A. Gladstone, Collector. *William A. Gladstone Afro-American Military Collection: Letter, raid of 54th Massachusetts and 2nd South Carolina, Combahee River, S.C., 5 June, 1863.* https://www.loc.gov/item/mss83434343/.

92. *Passengers on the Savannah Railroad, saw the blaze of burning property.*: "Yankee Raid at Combahee Ferry," *The Camden Confederate*, Camden, SC, June 5, 1863.

92. *The only thing left unscathed by roving soldiers was the slave quarters*: William L. Apthorp, "Montgomery's Raids in Florida, Georgia, and South Carolina;" Statement of William G. Heyward, respecting the Combahee raid. *Official History of the War of the Rebellion*, series 1, vol. xiv, 308; "The Raid on the Combahee," *The Times-Picayune*, (New Orleans, LA), June 28, 1863. I appreciate Ashley Council's assistance with research for this section on the raid.

93. *Mustering whatever strength was required*: Report of Capt. John F. Lay, G. 8. Army, Inspector of Cavalry, Hdqtrs. Dept. South Carolina, Georgia, and Florida, Charleston, 8. C. 7 June 24, 1863; *Official History of the War of the Rebellion*, series 1, vol. xiv, 303.

93. *their bundles and baskets perched on hips, shoulders, and heads, they brought with them squealing pigs and screaming chickens, dodging Confederate gunshots and the snapping jaws of angry dogs*: Bradford, *Scenes*, 38–42. Report of Capt. John F. Lay, 301.

93. *"Come Along! Come Along!"*: Bradford, *Harriet* (1901), 102.

94. *Her words were met with shouts of celebration and optimism*: "Harriet Tubman," *The Commonwealth* (Boston), July 10, 1863.

94. *"A Black She Moses"*: "Colonel Montgomery's Raid— The Rescued Black Chattels—A Black She 'Moses'— Her Wonderful Daring and Sagacity—The Black Regiments—Col. Higginson's Mistakes—Arrival of the 54th Massachusetts, &c., &c.," *Wisconsin State Journal* (Madison, WI), June 20, 1863.

94. *first woman, black or white, to plan and lead an armed military expedition during the Civil War*: "Colonel Montgomery's Raid," *Wisconsin State Journal*, June 20, 1863; "Harriet Tubman, *The Commonwealth*, July 10, 1863; Report of Brig. Gen. W. 8. Walker, C. 8. Army, commanding Third Military District Headquarters Third Military District, McPhersonville, June 17, 1863; *Official History of the War of the Rebellion*, series 1, vol. xiv; *Letter, raid of 54th Massachusetts and 2nd South Carolina, Combahee River, S.C., 5 June, 1863*.

To Die with Valor

96. *Lewis and Charles Douglass*: David W. Blight, *Frederick Douglass: Prophet of Freedom* (New York: Simon & Schuster, 2018).

98. "And when we saw the lightning, and that was the guns; and when we heard the thunder, and that was the big guns; and then we heard the rain falling, and that was the drops of blood falling; and when we came to get the crops, it was the dead we reaped": Albert Bushnell Hart, *Slavery and Abolition, 1831–1841, The American Nation: A History* (New York: Harper & Brothers Publishers, 1906), vol. 16, 209.

98. I'd go to the hospital, I would, early every morning. I'd get a big chunk of ice, I would, and put it in a basin, and fill it with water; then I'd take a sponge and begin. First man I'd come to, I'd thrash away the flies, and they'd arise, they would, like bees round a hive. Then I'd begin to bathe their wounds, and by the time I'd bathed off three or four, the fire and heat would have melted the ice and made the water warm, and it would be as red as clear blood. Then I'd go and get more ice, I would, and by the time I got to the next ones, the flies would be round de first ones, black and thick as ever.: Bradford, *Scenes*, 37. (Language changed to not rely on Bradford's interpretation of black dialect.)

98. *"I have now been absent two years almost, and have just got letters from my friends in Auburn, urging me to come home. My father and mother are old and in feeble health and need my care and attention."*: Conrad, *Harriet Tubman*, 181. Also see: Clinton, *Harriet Tubman*, 180.

99. *Harriet and her friends and family remained the legal property of their Maryland owners*: Maryland rewrites its state constitution ending slavery on November 1, 1864. *The Maryland Constitution of 1864*, Volume 667, 50.

100. *was given a furlough to travel to New York City and then to Boston*: Larson, *Bound for the Promised Land*, 226.

100. *Harriet was less than convinced by Truth's favorable opinion of their president*: Later in her life, Harriet supposedly changed her opinion about Lincoln, but in 1864, she was not a supporter of the president. See: Holt, "A Heroine in Ebony," 462.

PART IV: CALL ME MRS. DAVIS
A War Hero

107. *two and a half times that of white soldiers*: Larson, *Bound for the Promised Land*, 229. Also see: Tubman, Harriet, "Soldiers Dying From Hunger And Neglect, " *The Independent*, New York, July 27, 1865, 3, https://search-proquest-com.proxy.libraries.rutgers.edu/docview/90048820?accountid=13626.

Northern Realities

110. "copperhead scoundrel": (*a name hurled at Northern men and women who sympathized with the South*) *and reminded him that* "she didn't thank anybody to call her a colored person—She would be called black or Negro—she was as proud of being a black woman as he was of being white:" Martha Coffin Wright to Marianna Pelham Wright, November 7, 1865, Garrison Family Papers, Sophia Smith Collection, Smith College, Northampton, Massachusetts. Coffin wrote about this event directly after visiting with Harriet Tubman. Also see: Larson, *Bound for the Promised Land*, 232.

The Kindness of Strangers

111. *These accusations were difficult to confirm and ran counter to all of Harriet's previous actions but as the years wore on, a veil of mystery surrounding Margaret's arrival still lingered*: See, Larson, *Bound for the Promised Land*, 106–202; Clinton, *Harriet Tubman*, 117–123. For Brickler's account, see: Alice Lucas Brickler to Earl Conrad, July 19, 1939, Earl Conrad/Harriet Tubman Collection, New York Public Library, Schomburg Center for Research in Black Culture. Alice Lucas Brickler, Margaret's daughter, hurled the accusations of kidnapping against Harriet Davis. She stated that her mother had told her that her family was a well-situated free black family on the Eastern Shore of Maryland and that they had not given permission for Margaret's departure. Many historians have offered analysis about this story, however it's impossible to prove this accounting.

Tall, Dark, and Handsome

112. *He had been enslaved near Elizabeth City, North Carolina, but ran away to upstate New York sometime around 1861*: Calvin W. Mowbray and Maurice D. Rimpo, *Close-ups of Early Dorchester County History*, 63; Clinton, *Harriet Tubman*, 197.

112. *find his way from Brownsville, Texas, to Auburn, New York*: Clinton, *Harriet Tubman*, 198. Nelson traveled with another soldier who was from upstate New York.

113. *Harriet's first husband died*: "Outrage in Talbot County. A Colored Man Murdered," *Baltimore News American* (Baltimore, MD), October 7, 1867. Also see: Larson, *Bound for the Promised Land*, 240.

114. "That Vincent murdered the deceased we presume no one doubts; but as no one but a colored boy saw him commit the deed, it was universally conceded that he would be acquitted, the moment it was ascertained that the jury was composed exclusively of Democrats.": "Acquittal of a Murderer," *Cambridge Intelligencer* (Cambridge, MD), December 23, 1867, quoted in Jean McMahon Humez, *Harriet Tubman: The Life and the Life Stories* (Madison: University of Wisconsin Press, 2003), 77.

116. *Harriet's denied request and her recent difficulties appeared in* The National Anti-Slavery Standard: Letter from Sallie Holley, *National Anti-Slavery Standard*, Washington, DC, November 30, 1867. Also see: Larson, *Bound for the Promised Land*, 241.

Telling Her Story

117. "The difference between us is very marked, Most that I have done and suffered in the service of our cause has been in public, and I have received much encouragement at every step of the way. You, on the other hand, have labored in a private way.": Frederick Douglass to Harriet Tubman, August 29, 1868, quoted in full in Bradford, *Scenes*, 7–8.

A Wife and Mother

118. *wedding as a large celebration with many friends and well-known families of Auburn.*: Tubman-Davis Wedding Notice, *Auburn Morning News*, Auburn, NY, March 19, 1869.

119. *was not one to abandon a mission.*: See: Mr. McDougall, House of Representatives of the United States Forty-Third Congress, H.R. 2711. Harriet once again applied for a pension in 1874.

Hard Times

120. *Nelson was heavily involved in St. Mark's AME Church and eventually became a trustee.*: Humez, *Harriet Tubman*, 92.

121. *That now included a daughter named Gertie.*: According to the 1875 census, Gertie is listed as adopted in the Tubman household, and, in the 1880 federal census, she is identified as Harriet and Nelson's daughter. See: Larson, *Bound for the Promised Land*, 260.

121. *swindled out of money*: For more on Harriet being swindled, see: Humez, *Harriet Tubman*, 88-90.

Mother Tubman

126. *in 1896 the National Association of Colored Women was founded.*: On the founding of the NACW and the organization's ideology and activism: Deborah G. White, *Too Heavy a Load: Black Women in Defense of Themselves, 1894–1994* (New York: W. W. Norton, 1999). Also see: Rosalyn Terborg-Penn, *African American Women in the Struggle for the Vote, 1850–1920* (Bloomington: Indiana University Press, 1998).

126. a *home and hospital for elderly and invalid black people.*: "Official Minutes of the National Federation of Afro-American Women Held in Washington, DC, July 20, 21, 22, 1896," National Association of Colored Women's Clubs, Washington, DC, 1902. Also see: Larson, *Bound for the Promised Land*, 275.

Getting Paid

128–129. *Harriet was awarded twenty dollars per month, eight dollars for her widow's pension and twelve dollars for her service as a nurse.*: US House of Representatives, Tubman/Davis Pension File, Fifty-Fifth Congress, Third Session, report no. 1619.

Servant of God

133. *"I go away to prepare a place for you, that where I am you also may be."*: "Death of Aunt Harriet, 'Moses of Her People,'" *Auburn Daily Advertiser* (Auburn, NY), March 11, 1913.

134. *"tell the women to stand together for God will never forsaken [sic] us."*: "Mrs. Talbert's Tribute," *Auburn Citizen*, March 14, 1913, 5. Also see: Larson, *Bound for the Promised Land*, 289.

ACKNOWLEDGMENTS

I am a fortunate woman. I have the great privilege of reading and writing about the lives of black women (enslaved and free) for a living. It's been my life's mission to tease the stories of my subjects from the margins of the archives. I always start each research project with great excitement and hope. I know that my subjects aren't hidden, they are simply waiting to be found.

I stand in deep admiration of Harriet Tubman Davis. I hope that I have written a biography of her that is accessible and gives everyone an opportunity to know more about one of the fiercest women to ever walk the planet. I am deeply indebted to the Tubman biographers who have contributed a wealth of information about the life of the woman also known as Moses. Kate Clifford Larson and Catherine Clinton were both generous with their time and shared their insights with me. Throughout the twentieth and twenty-first centuries, Jean Humez, Beverly Lowry, Lois Horton, Milton Sernett, Earl Conrad, and Emma P. Telford have all contributed important scholarship about Tubman. I am indebted to them and their work.

I had two wonderful research assistants who helped me shepherd this book to completion. William Harrison Graves and Ashley Council are stellar graduate students who handled the intensity of this project with grace and style.

Monica Ahanonu's illustrations breathe new life into Tubman's story. I am grateful for her imagination and her beautiful artwork that help tell an almost unbelievable tale. As I worked to collect rare photos of Tubman I leaned on the generosity of several institutions. The Smithsonian National Museum of African American History and Culture, the Library of Congress, the National Archives, the Boston Athenæum, the American Civil War Museum, the National Portrait Gallery, the Schomburg Center for Research in Black Culture, and the American Antiquarian Society all provided wonderful access to images and newspapers necessary for this book.

As always, I thank my family for putting up with my crankiness during the writing of this book. Jeff and Christian—I love y'all. And thanks to my agent, Laura Dail, who is my biggest advocate and thoughtful confidante. Finally, I must thank my editor, Dawn Davis, who was the inspiration behind this project. Whenever I work with Dawn I am overwhelmed by her talent and keen eye. Thank you for inviting me to ride with you.

The redesign of the twenty-dollar bill featuring Harriet Tubman
that was slotted for a 2020 unveiling has been delayed.
As of this writing, there are no plans to unveil the new bill before 2028.